Notes & Blots

from a psychologist's desk

Marvin Rosen

Notes & Blots

from a psychologist's desk

Nelson-Hall nh Chicago

Library of Congress Cataloging in Publication Data

Rosen, Marvin.
   Notes & blots from a psychologist's desk.

   Bibliography: p. 205
   Includes index.
   1.   Clinical psychology—Addresses, essays,
lectures.   I.   Title.
RC467.R56   157′,9   77-16183
ISBN 0-88229-199-8

Manufactured in the United States of America.

10   9   8   7   6   5   4   3   2   1

Contents

Preface

To some, the clinical psychologist is an omnipotent guru, tuned into one's innermost thoughts and capable of effecting miraculous transformations of personality by means of powerful, unspoken magic. To others he is a professional busybody, complicating basic human relationships with the latest fad in psychological treatment. Although some psychologists may unwittingly perpetuate both stereotypes, each represents a distortion of reality.

In writing this book, it was my intention to present a more realistic account of the thinking and techniques of clinical psychologists. Various chapters present descriptive accounts of assessment, psychotherapy, behavioral research, and theoretical conceptions, often with little continuity. These areas were chosen because they reflect a broad range of functions, activities, and roles assumed by psychologists. Not every psychologist engages in every activity depicted in this volume. Collectively, clinical psychologists do all these things and more.

Despite the variety of topics included, a unifying theme exists in the basic trust psychologists place in the empirical method for generating knowledge, validating theory, and evaluating the effectiveness of their methods. No other professional group seems as self-critical, as driven to challenge their own ideas, and as willing to subject their methods to experimental test.

Anyone who has mistakenly enrolled in an introductory college level psychology course seeking "self-understanding," soon learns how jealously psychology guards its scientific tradition. Whether we function within the "ivory tower," the industrial setting, or the mental health clinic, most of us owe a deeper allegiance to Pavlov, Thorndike, Woodworth, and Watson, than to Freud.

Yet, psychology also has its subjective side. For all our faith in what is scientific and objective, empirically demonstrable, and statistically established, we need to deal with people. We practice psychotherapy. We relate. We intuit. We speculate about the behaviors that we observe. And sometimes, throwing caution to the winds, we analyze and synthesize from within the depths of our own gut reactions in ways we never learned in school.

Psychologists study human and animal behavior. Some psychologists choose to specialize in abnormal or deviant behavior. They may teach courses in psychopathology at colleges or universities. They may conduct research designed to reveal basic facts about the causes or nature of mental disorders. They may develop simple or elegant theories about behavior and publish their ideas in professional journals. Or, they may be practitioners at hospitals, clinics, schools, institutions or in private practice. In no instance, can their work be divorced from the basic processes of learning, motivation, emotion, perception, and thinking, which comprise the science of psychology.

This book was not intended to serve as a textbook in clinical psychology. Rather, it was written for the interested layman seeking a realistic appraisal of what clinical psychologists do, and what clinical psychology is all about. It is a book that I would have wanted to read as an undergraduate contemplating a career in psychology. The book was written twice. Initially, it was a rather dull collection of previously published journal papers. I am grateful to Mrs. Jean Horton Berg, who encouraged me to re-write it in a more popular style, using the original version as source material. To this end, references were removed from the text. Relevant background material is referenced after every chapter.

In retrospect, I find that the autobiographical style has imposed a highly personal view of psychology. Hopefully, what has been lost in objectivity will be offset by the validity of the experiences presented. The names of clients used in case study descriptions have been changed to maintain anonymity. The names of faculty members at the University of Pennsylvania, during the time I attended, have also been disguised. For any injustices in these descriptions, I apologize. It is to these teachers and friends that I am most indebted for the role models they provided.

1

Awakening the Dead

The large gold letters on the heavy oak door grandly announced ARCHIVES, but the room was seldom used except for meetings. One wall was lined with glass-enclosed shelves stretching from floor to ceiling and overladen with crumbling journals, dusty old textbooks, and decaying memorabilia reflecting a century and a quarter of the history of an institution. On the far wall, within spanking new display cases, were a set of dolls salvaged from the dustheap. The placard read Circa 1870. An ancient grandfather clock, the pride of the librarian who dutifully keywound it each morning, chimed the hour. Around the walls were the distinguished portraits of those who had played their roles as institutional leaders, public benefactors, and community advocates of the mentally retarded. Dorothea Dix flashed the same righteous indignation she must have shown in her impassioned plea to the legislature of Massachusetts in 1848. Half a dozen other patriarchs were labeled with names that are familiar on hospitals and schools across the country.

Few readers wandered in to browse and those who did seldom ventured beyond the mock-ups from the ancient object rooms where children, sheltered from a

world they could not understand, learned of a post office from a miniature model. But I had access to the
keys and loved to spend an idle hour rummaging
through dusty manuscripts reading what my predeces-
sors a hundred years removed had had to say. It all was
there for anyone who cared to take the time to read: the
yellowed annual reports in which the superintendents
and department heads described their programs and
appealed for support. The journals of the hallowed
Association, founded here a hundred years ago. The
early handwritten student records exhaustively described every child with ample evidence of the pre-
sumed causes of their debilitating wretchedness in sins
passed down (they said) through generations of intem-
perance and sloth. An ancient steel cabinet housed
photographs of what the campus looked like with all
the monster dormitories which we tore down five years
ago. Some tattered, dog-eared vintage plates from
1865, or so, depicted what photography was like in its
infancy.

I must have read five thousand pages or more
about Itard, who tried to teach the "wild boy" Victor
and thought he'd failed. And about Seguin, who found
a way to treat Parisian "idiots." The physiologic method
meant sensory stimulation by endless repetitions of
sounds and sights and smells and tireless manipulations
of the muscles.

Richards came to Philadelphia and started up a
school. His second annual report to the esteemed Board
of Directors describes his work with some poor, helpless five-year old who could neither walk nor talk. By
reading to the child as if he were intelligent, Richards
hoped to make a dent. And, if he noted some minute
flutter of the eyes whenever reading stopped, he knew
the boy attended.

Unfortunately, this optimism was not long-standing. Schools were soon so overcrowded that the cries to economize drowned out the few who still clung to their early hopes to teach and train. Samuel Gridley Howe was dead, and Seguin also had been eulogized. The school became the institution. Genetics reared its scientific head, and studies of the Jukes and Kallikaks confirmed that mental deficiency was really to blame for crime. "There is a dangerous element in our midst," cried one illustrious leader. "The menace of the retarded." And people read his book. So these "elements" were segregated to protect our land from further pollution of the stock. Eugenic measures were the order of the day. A lot of sterilizations were done in California. And mental tests were now available to prove stupidity was irreversible. A child of twelve whose brain has shown three years' growth, can never learn what four-year olds can, so they said. And when a scientist took defective children from an orphanage, and stimulated them, and showed that their IQs elevated, and showed that those who stayed behind remained behind, and presented his well-drawn graphs and charts to a learned body of authorities, they crucified him.

But people did leave institutions. Some ran away. Some others left on "parole." Social workers visited some who left and reported back to medical superintendents on how well they did. Some made good soldiers at Bastogne and Tobruk. Others who were placed in factories made the boots and guns. It could no longer be denied that not all of the mentally retarded required the institution. So parents' groups grew militant and knocked upon the doors in Washington. And Congress responded.

"Normalization," cried the Scandinavians. "De-

institutionalization," demanded those who'd been
outraged by purgatories previously called Training
Schools. Basic human rights, due process, right to
education, and institutional peonage became the new
catchwords of change.

I wrote a letter to ten publishers. "Why not a
book?" I asked. "Collected Papers" to trace the history
of mental retardation. Let people read the way we've
treated those who once were called "Les enfants du Bon
Dieu." Nine publishers replied that it didn't quite fit
into their plans for the year. One called up and said
O.K. "We're starting a new series this year. This is
what we've been looking for."

The Xerox machine was made to order for
reproducing from old manuscripts. The pages crumbled
in my fingers, and I knew that in another decade there'd
be nothing left to reproduce. I breathed the dust of
history that year and, like Lazarus, reawakened sleeping giants of the past. I found them all. So Dix and
Howe and Seguin and Binet and all the rest were given
one more chance to howl. I wrote some filler to tie it all
together and spent two weeks proofreading galleys
until my eyes were red, and made an index. ". . . a
panorama of Western civilization's concepts, philosophy and practice in the treatment of mental retardation . . ." the flier read. Complete in two volumes. Out
in December. I worried over what reviewers would say.

To put a book together from the papers of others
requires time, compulsive attention to detail, and a
Xerox machine. The book was done, and copies sent
around to relatives and friends. A few libraries would
purchase it and stack it in some dingy corner. Perhaps
some college profs who trained others to do what they
didn't do so well would make assignments from volume one.

I wondered if I might someday try again and write one all myself. Now, wouldn't it be grand to do a book about the practice of psychology today and how I work at it . . . ?

2

Killing Oneself by Degrees

Philadelphia was hot and sticky that summer of 1956. Following the green arrows, I found my way from the 30th Street Station to the Subway Surface Car, which would take me to the campus of the University of Pennsylvania. At 36th Street, I paid the motorman, made my exit, and climbed the dimly lit stairs to street level. The sign said "Spruce Street", and I knew I had arrived. Across from the station the massive brick structures, flanking the entrance to a large court yard, were obviously dormitories. Farther down the street, I could make out the clinic entrance of the University Hospital. Not far from the subway exit, I entered an imposing building to ask directions. I found I was in Houston Hall, the Student Union, and a tweedy, buttoned-down instructor pointed me directly through the building to the college quadrangle. College Hall, my destination, seemed a run-down facsimile of the ivy-covered towers where I had spent my undergraduate years.

The psychology department occupied rather inauspicious quarters in the basement. It consisted of two large communal offices, including a newly dedicated departmental library, in which instructors, graduate-student teachers, and research assistants were crowded desk to desk. At the west end of the building was the historic Psychological Clinic.

I made myself known to Dr. Zeits, the department chairman, and was shown the desk to be used in my capacity as half-time teaching assistant. In return for keeping track of attendance, scoring examinations, and assisting with equipment for laboratory demonstrations, I was to receive six hundred dollars and my tuition.

I aspired to a doctorate degree in psychology, and my interest was in clinical psychology. I wanted to work in a helping relationship with people, particularly with children. I had completed an undergraduate major in psychology at Cornell and felt well prepared to continue my studies at the school where the first American Psychological Clinic had been founded. Whatever grand ideas I entertained about psychology were soon to be reshaped. Psychology at Penn was a far cry from Sigmund Freud.

The instincts and their vicissitudes, which had so intrigued me as an undergraduate, seemed alien to the faculty at Penn. We spent our days debating whether rats turn right or left by learning stimulus-response associations or relationships in space. Such questions, we were told, were very significant.

The top floor of Hare Building, a few short yards away, housed the animal laboratories. DO NOT ENTER. EXPERIMENT IN PROGRESS signs screamed from the doors. It was here that the frontiers of science were to be expanded. Psychology had found its answers, not from consulting rooms and armchair speculation, but from empiricism, the very fount of knowledge. The gods we came to worship were surely to be found among the shiny cages, well-marked charts, relay racks, Skinner boxes, digital counters, event recorders, and squiggley lines scratching paths of truth on revolving rolls of paper. Casting off all hints of subjectivity, psychology became a science. We were there to learn its many mysteries.

Graduate work required an equal mixture of drudgery and anxiety. The seminars demanded that an enormous amount of reading be digested. Every available hour was devoted to library work. Most of the material appeared in psychological journals which were placed "on reserve" for us. Term papers, seminar presentations, and examinations became a way of life.

The most formidable hurdle lay before us. "Prelims"—qualifying examinations taken after the second year of study—covered all basic areas of psychology and statistics and were required for acceptance to the doctoral program. It was department policy to accept a large first year class, knowing that there would be attrition. Inevitably, the anxiety level increased as the time for the examination drew near. By the end of the second year panic took hold, and life became unbearable. Once the ordeal was over, however, the pressure was removed. Having passed his "prelims," the student achieved a degree of status in the department, and it was generally assumed that ultimately the doctorate degree would be awarded. "Ultimately" was ambiguously defined.

The major obstacle during the first year was a survey of all areas of psychology in a course called the "pro-sem". Each department member presented his major area of specialization. We were also required to enroll in a statistics course, as well as a seminar dealing with the history of psychology. An additional seminar was to be of our own choosing. It was further expected that we would make ourselves available to a faculty member to assist in a research project and to begin developing our own research ideas.

Personality seminar, for example, was an historical presentation of thinking and research dating from the ancient Greeks. The term "personality" derives from the Greek word "persona," meaning "mask," or "to sound through," and relates to the masks worn by actors in Greek drama. One meaning of personality is the role played by the individual in life. The seminar covered various questions of theory and research: Is there a consistency of personality over the years so that various traits and attributes remain relatively stable over time? Are traits such as honesty general in nature, or do some people act honestly in some situations but not in others? What are the units of personality—traits, habits or typologies? To what extent does body type contribute to personality? What are the major theoretical models by which we can account for the personality data?

We read Freud and Maslow and Allport. We oriented our thinking and aligned our prejudices. There was little support in the department for dynamic interpretations. A student learned quickly of the prejudice of behaviorists toward the subjective, untestable, intuitive. "If it cannot be measured, it doesn't exist." Other departments allowed room for humanistic approaches. At Penn there was the cold objectivity of scientific empiricism. It was only in later years that I felt safe enough to question the god of statistical inference as the ultimate criterion and to place some trust in personal intuition and clinical insight.

Somehow most of us survived the first year. The

second year proved more relevant for majors in clinical psychology and, despite the spectre of "prelims" at the conclusion of the spring semester, my year would have been unblemished had it not been interrupted that summer by six months of active duty with the Army Reserve.

The transition from the ivied walls of College Hall to the chaotic Fort Dix Induction Center was traumatic, and the ordeal of basic training need not be elaborated here. By Christmas I had served my time and returned to school. I was determined that the lost six months would not set me back. With reckless confidence I committed myself to the "prelim" examination in the spring.

But first, there were the second year seminars. The major ones, for my purposes, were Wishner's *Psychopathology*, and Jones' *Motivation*. Psychopathology was a compendium of research in broad areas of abnormal behavior. The major clinical syndromes were considered both from a clinical and an experimental viewpoint.

Schizophrenia was a major concern. Wishner had formulated a theory of efficiency to account for schizophrenic behavior. Schizophrenics, he reasoned, were diffuse and inefficient in their response, unable to focus their behavior upon specific task requirements. Physiological measures of muscular tension were used to measure focused and diffuse behavior. Psychiatric patients were found to be more diffuse in their muscular response than normal persons; psychotics were more diffuse than neurotics. Several of my classmates spent the better part of their graduate school careers reading muscle-action potentials from miles of recording paper and developing research studies to validate and extend Wishner's efficiency theory.

Monthly graduate colloquia provided additional

stimulation. Distinguished psychologists from other universities were invited to present seminars for faculty and graduate students. Festinger, Bitterman, Spence, Bruner. We heard them all, and later basked in their brilliance at cocktails and dinner, if pocketbooks allowed. These meetings were fascinating exhibitions of verbal and intellectual dueling. Department members sharpened their claws in preparation, and at times were over-zealous in their attack on a visiting speaker. Each faculty member seemed determined to outdo the other; and graduate students often joined in the onslaught. Many a speaker was visibly shaken if unable to rebuff a challenge or defend some hidden bias in his research design.

We learned well in these colloquia—perhaps too well. The critical attitude was so deeply imprinted that it became our style to criticize and tear apart. So accustomed were we to finding fault that our own creative efforts were often stifled by intimidation and self-doubt.

I passed my "prelims" in the spring of 1957. The weeks of preparation were a nightmare of grinding toil. Each area of psychology was represented in two full days of written examinations. The amount of material to be digested and committed to memory was staggering. To expedite matters, I wrote brief answers to hypothetical questions on index cards and tacked them on my bedroom walls. Before very long the walls were solidly covered with vital information I alone could understand. The night before the test I read my walls from window ledge to closet door. I knew there'd be few surprises the next day.

I had no doubt that I had clobbered the exam and was not anxious on the day results were posted. I did well in all areas. The following year I also passed examinations in major and minor areas of concentration, but never distinguished myself as well as on the "prelims."

My teaching assistantship required that I teach recitation sections and laboratories during my second and third years. Sometimes I was asked to lecture to large undergraduate classes. I enjoyed pacing back and forth in front of a class, filling one blackboard after another with diagrams, terms, dates, and names, timing my presentation so that I had completely encircled the room by the time the hour was over. I learned psychology by teaching it and have kept my hand in teaching ever since.

On one occasion I might better have remained in bed. My subject was "The Oedipus complex and its importance to the psychoanalytic conception of personality development." I hoped to be explicit about what Freud really meant. Well armed with juicy instances of incestuous desires of mothers, fathers, daughters, and sons, I spread my notes before me on the lectern and waited for the group to quiet down. To my chagrin, I found my audience to be more than the usual yawning undergraduates. It was Parents' Day, and the hall was filled to overflowing with forty portly moms and dads, proudly flanking grinning offspring, and waiting patiently to hear what words of wisdom I might spew forth. They wanted to learn firsthand what their tuition checks were purchasing.

Somehow I stumbled through my notes, choking over "penis envy," "castration anxiety," and the like, and watched the hour hand overhead crawl slowly around until the final bell. At last the hour was over, and as I tried to get away somewhere to lick my wounds, a prosperous looking gentleman cut off my exit route. "Here it comes," I thought. "Probably some

influential almnus type." "PSYCHOLOGY IN-
STRUCTOR CENSORED," the headlines would pro-
nounce. I hastily constructed my defense, mumbling,
"It's Freud that had the dirty mind."

"Great work," he beamed. "I'm an analyst, you
know. Didn't think they taught such things in college.
Just wanted to shake your hand."

I muttered some ridiculous response and floated
slowly back to earth.

My hand shook as I handed the Department Chairman a pen. Dramatically he drew out the moment, then
scrawled his narcissistic signature across the neatly
type-written page.

"Valence, Expectancy, and Dissonance Reduction
in the Prediction of Achievement Striving"

Marvin Rosen

A Dissertation in Psychology

Presented to the Faculty of the Graduate School
of the University of Pennsylvania in Partial
Fulfillment of the Requirements for the Degree
of Doctor of Philosophy.

1961

I grinned with relief as the chairman shook my
hand. I had only to present the signed manuscript to the
Graduate School Office, and it was done.

For an entire year I had worked. The fifty-two page
paper, not including tables, scarcely conveyed what
really had transpired. Sure, the procedures were explic-
itly described, and the rationale, (the antecedents of my
thoughts), well documented by year, volume, and page.
The results were there in detail—each laboriously

examined and statistically evaluated—but not the toil, worry, and obsessional concern with counterbalancing, subject matching, and bias that might be unforeseen in the data.

The study was completed after several months of data analysis, write-up, and rewriting. I learned something about writing. On one version of my repeated drafts of the paper, my dissertation chairman scrawled across the front page: "There is no substitute for a simple declarative sentence." In any event, I received my Ph.D., went on to an internship, clinical jobs, teaching, and other research. However, once completed, the dissertation aroused considerable aversive motivation on my part. I made two abortive attempts at publication while at the Veterans' Administration. The *Journal of Abnormal and Social Psychology* felt the study was obvious and unimportant. The *Journal of Personality* was likewise unimpressed. My dissertation chairman described my study in his book but was disappointed at my lack of industry at getting the results into literature. I had become involved in other things and allowed my discouragement and satiation with the dissertation to overwhelm my motivation to pursue it further. It sits today in three places—on a top shelf in my office, in the University of Pennsylvania Library, and as a microfilmed Dissertation Abstract available from the University of Michigan.

3
The Old Man of the Mountain

I sat across the table from the lanky student and tried to size him up. His flat, accent-free speech gave no hint of his origins. His was just another face among the hundreds I was teaching, as part of my graduate school assistantship. When I asked for a volunteer to serve as a subject while I learned to use the Rorschach, Joe raised his hand. "I'm a psychology major," he said. "Might want to go to graduate school. Like to see firsthand what it's all about." I took his name, arranged a time and place, and did not think of Joe till he appeared again, eager to begin.

The Rorschach plates were neatly stacked beside me. I had a pad and pencil to record his verbal responses; a stopwatch would reveal how fast he reacted to each of the ten inkblot stimulus cards.

"This is a test of imagination," I explained, trying to assume a professional role. "There are no right or wrong answers. I just want to see what these blots look like to you. Tell me whatever they remind you of, no matter how silly or unimportant it might seem."

Projective tests are procedures that utilize relatively unstructured, ambiguous test stimuli. The individual being evaluated is asked to react to the stimuli in various ways; for example, to describe what he sees, draw a picture, make up a story, or complete an incomplete sentence. Since the stimuli are relatively amorphous, it is assumed that the individual expresses something personal about himself in the manner in which he responds and in the content of his response. Because the possibilities of response are almost infinite, the tests are a potentially rich source of information, presumably related to meaningful dynamics of personality.

Projective tests are not "tests" in the strict sense of the term, since their validity for predicting relevant criteria of functioning has not been well established. Rather, the procedures are more an art than a science. The inferences drawn represent a set of descriptive hypotheses about personality rather than established test findings.

Psychologists either believe in projective tests or they don't. Those who do, believe that test responses reflect dimensions of personality useful in diagnosis or therapy, and that projective responses represent a sample of behavior predictive of responses in other situations.

Most hard-nosed, empirically-oriented psychologists restrict themselves to better validated, objective tests of personality, or to the analysis and measurement of observable behaviors. Such methods are more accurate (reliable), but provide a more constricted range of information, since the opportunities for response are limited. One psychologist described projective testing as similar to the reception of a radio receiver with wide band width but poor fidelity.

The Rorschach, or inkblot test, is one of the most widely used and most controversial of projective test procedures. Analysis is based upon several factors, which include the specific blot characteristics used by the subject, the accuracy of his response compared to published norms, the number of responses, the frequency of different kinds of responses, and the content of the imagery expressed by the subject.

"Here's the first card, Joe. Just tell me what you see."

"Well, let's see. It's the body of an angel. The hands are lifted up to heaven. You're not supposed to turn it around are you?"

"Hold it any way you like." I scrawled his answer on my pad and marked it number one. "What made it look that way to you?"

"Her hands and thumb and fingers. She doesn't have much of a head. There's her waist."

What was the special meaning of an angel to Joe? He might have said a thousand things that would have fit the form. Did heaven have some strange appeal? Was he preoccupied with guilt or sin that his figures had to pray? My associations outraced his. She had a waist but not a head. The waist separates sexual areas from that part of the body which represents intellectual control. Was Joe having problems controlling sexual impulses? He asked to turn the card around.

"Hold on," I cautioned myself. "One response and you've already got him diagnosed. Go on with the test."

"Looks like an alligator's head right here. The head and eye. Cut off the top right here."

"What else?"

"The whole thing looks just like a sea . . . what do you call those things with the little tail? A sea horse. Here's his snout and curvy body."

I led Joe carefully through each of the nine remaining cards.

"I have to admit this card reminds me of an old snatch. This black and white part. It looks kind of hairy. It's got kind of a clitoris up here. This looks like the old man of the mountain. There's his nose, chin, and eye. This thing is a mountain with a man's face carved out of it. This reminds me of an Asian. More like a Buddhist statue now. His hat and face and shoulders rounding out. These are two red seals. They're sitting out and talking to one another on an ice floe. Shaped like a seal with a big ass and long neck flippers."

"There's a couple of men here, and each has a hold of a magnetic hemisphere, and they are trying to separate them by yanking. No, it's a couple of females. I'm sorry."

"What made you change your mind?"

"Hard to tell, cause it's got a breast up here and a penis down here. But the heads look like females. Both are leaning back trying to get their weight into pulling this apart. . . . There's a butterfly flying through the middle. It's got two red wings shaped like butterfly wings. It's detached from everything else as a unit . . . makes it look like a single butterfly."

"There's a couple of vultures out there looking things over. This one's got a beak and his head is drooping down like he's looking down on the ground for something to grab. There's a walrus sticking his head out of a cave. This looks like a map of Cape Cod. Jagged coast here, semi-circular. A big fat guy is sitting on top of this walrus going for a ride in the snow. He's got a fur coat on and it's zipped up tight to his neck."

After we were finished, I thanked Joe for his help. Whatever conclusions I drew from his record, I would be sure to maintain his anonymity. The record remained several weeks among a pile of papers on my desk, one of several assignments awaiting completion. Eventually I scored the responses and organized my thoughts into a coherent report, which would surely satisfy my obligation for the assignment. I speculated about Joe's guilt and feelings of depression. What was his terrible secret? Was Joe really the "old man of the mountain?" Did he see himself as eroded, close to dying? And what about his sexual confusion? Was Joe depressed because of homosexual concerns? Why had he volunteered to take this test? He knew I was a student, inexperienced. Could he be seeking help? Should I refer him to the Student Counseling Service? "Forget it," I reassured myself. "Why worry about such phantasy? An interesting exercise. That's all it is. Unproven. Not a test at all." I submitted my report and went on to more pressing matters.

It was only a two line "obit" in the *Inquirer*, but the campus was abuzz with it. Joe killed himself on Tuesday—locked the door of his garage and turned the engine on.

4

Journeying in the Other World

"When a person finds himself in a total impasse, if he does not commit suicide, nature sometimes calls upon a healing process that has been available to mankind at all times and in all places. . . . I refer to the ceremonies of initiation practiced all over the world until very recently, when a person was conducted through an experience of (1) death; of (2) journeying in the Other World; of (3) rebirth from that Place and that Time back into this world with its here and now. Schizophrenia is a confused attempt to conduct such a sequence" (Laing, 1967).

With clothing, books, and record player crammed tight in the back seat of the Pontiac, I started the short two-hour trip along Route 40 to Perryville. The internship year, necessary for completion of my training, was about to begin.

The town turned out to be a few run-down stores, a firehouse, and a bar. The Veterans Administration Hospital, which provided employment for many of the locals, stretched out on a point of land jutting into Chesapeake Bay. During the winter months, a cold fog crept in from the ocean and blended land and sky in a desolate shade of grey. During the summer, a small marina along the water's edge attracted boaters and fishermen for miles around, and the hospital pall was lessened with their presence. A winding two-lane road connected the sprawling hospital area with the town. A uniformed guard at the entrance suspiciously eyed each approaching vehicle. There could be no mistaking the fact that the many two-story brick structures, each with its own screened-in veranda, concealed the wards of a mental hospital. Just beyond the entrance, the approach road led under a Pennsylvania Railroad trestle. One Halloween eve, I was to learn later, a patient had laid his head upon the tracks in the path of an oncoming express. The head severed clean and rolled down the embankment in full view of drivers entering the hospital, who, thinking it a grotesque Halloween prank, left it where it lay.

Employees were housed in a stony structure set apart from the patient area, not far from the water's edge. Nurses, physicians, and psychologists were quartered here in two adjacent wings, one male and one female. A social worker (of uncertain sexual persuasion), kept an apartment squarely centered between the two wings, a location I regarded as especially appropriate at the time. It was in this building that I was to spend the next fifteen months, learning what neither textbook nor university professor could provide.

W. Horsely Gantt, my next door neighbor, was a Pavlovian psychologist, well known for studies of experimental neuroses in animals. Although in his seventies, Gantt was a healthy, vigorous man. A strong advocate of physical conditioning, he was accustomed to a brisk walk or a bicycle ride each morning before breakfast. I was told he was a polar bear and given to frigid, midwinter dips in the bay. Religiously, each morning at 6:00 A.M., I was jolted awake by the stirring strains of "Bringing in the Sheaves," emanating from his turntable and vibrating my furniture through our common wall.

The Psychology Department consisted of a half-dozen staff members and an equal number of interns from surrounding universities. They engaged in the usual hospital duties of psychologists—evaluation and diagnosis, group and individual psychotherapy, and participation in interdisciplinary treatment "teams" within the hospital wards. Interns shared the work load of staff psychologists, but were closely supervised. Weekly seminars were provided to allow us to present our therapy cases. A consulting psychoanalyst from Baltimore chaired these seminars, and over a period of several months, I presented one of my cases at this meeting. Dr. Dryface commented upon the patient's personality dynamics and monitored my performance as a therapist. The conference was well attended, and I gained some local notoriety as a consequence of my bumbling efforts.

Nelly T. was a forty-five year old nurse from the hills of Tennessee. She was diagnosed as manic-depressive, and I was to see both phases of her illness before I was through. Nelly had a history of post-partum depressions, suicide attempts, and a recent divorce. Because of the pressure of case presentations, I needed to take copious notes of her verbalizations and my responses during therapy. During her manic state, she provided me with ample ammunition for my meeting. My notes were pregnant with sexual invitations, angry challenges, agressive outbursts, and other "loaded" material that provided Dr. Dryface a rich opportunity for interpretation.

"How are you, Doctor? What took you so long

today? I've been waiting all morning for you to come. I brought us coffee and donuts. Let's have a picnic. I used to love picnics when I was young. Everything from soup to nuts. Do you think I'm nuts? We're all nuts here. If you were cooped up with the women on this wing, you'd be nuts too. Hey, I bet if we locked the door, we could really have some fun."

"Nelly, you know that's not why I come to see you."

"Why do you come, then? You really don't care about me. You're just like all the rest. If you really want to help, why don't you get me out of here? Just leave your keys behind when you go. I'll do the rest. What I need is a good belt of bourbon. How about bringing me a bottle the next time you come? We can have a ball."

Several months later Nelly entered the depressive phase of her disorder. Her talking slowed down to the minimum amount required in response to my questions. Finally, it ceased entirely. With encouragement from the analyst, I waited out her long silence, stoically reassuring Nelly that I would remain with her through her torment, even though she couldn't talk to me. Nelly tried valiantly to rid herself of me during this time, but I tenaciously hung on, interpreting her silence when I had nothing else to say. My notes dwindled to nothing, and I was becoming increasingly uncomfortable with Dr. Dryface.

"What do I do now?" I pleaded at the conference. "She's not saying anything. We just sit and look at each other"

"Be patient," Dr. Dryface advised. So for hour after hour, I was Job.

"It's raining," Nelly observed, looking towards the window. Gratefully, I wrote it down.

"What did she say today?" Dr. Dryface queried, hopefully.

"She said it was raining."

"The patient is sad," he interpreted sagely. "It brings to mind a French poem from my childhood. '*Il pleure dans mon coeur comme il pleure sur la ville.*' It rains in my heart as it rains on the city."

"It really *was* raining, Doctor. Thundering and lightning too. I had to shut the window."

"That's hardly relevant, young man. The weather notwithstanding, your patient is crying. In French the same word expresses both meanings, you know."

"How much longer is she going to rain, Doctor? I'm not helping Nelly."

I continued to see Nelly, and eventually she did talk again. I don't know if I helped her much that year, but I walked with her through darkness so intense that neither she nor I could find the way.

Not all the patients were depressed. A burly mechanic feared being poisoned and believed that mice talked to him; an asthenic black man had sodomized an eight year old girl; an attractive WAC was having crying spells and headaches subsequent to her divorce; a confused purple heart holder had brandished a gun and was being charged with assault and intent to kill.

They poured out their tales with little provocation. A marine sergeant detailed the horrors of his combat patrols on Iwo Jima and Saipan. With slowly increasing effect, he climaxed his story in paroxysms of uncontrollable sobbing.

A neurotic housewife found everything painful and tiring. She complained of back pain, a cold, nervousness, fatigue, pins and needles, and St. Vitus' Dance.

"I don't feel a bit better than when I came in. I shouldn't be taking this test today. I don't feel too well."

A roly-poly secretary in tight toreador slacks squealed in delight at my test questions: "A plant comes from a teeny, eeny, eeny seed. Absolutely gorgeous."

A suspicious and negative trial lawyer threw his pencil down, expressed doubt that anyone could solve the problems in my book, then challenged me to try.

A flirtatious school teacher became teasingly provocative: "I've heard the test can tell whether or not a woman is a virgin. Did you think I was going to see something interesting? That looks like the bag of a cow, but I know you wouldn't have such things."

My interpretations to test responses were often incisive, naive, symbolic, descriptive, clever, commonplace, insightful, or trite. "Open mouths" and "ice cream cones" and "cocktail glasses,"—the patients obligingly responded to twelve ink-splattered cards. "Strong oral dependent needs," I instantly concluded, for I had learned my lessons well. One badly frightened soul vividly described "the face of a man with a large mouth that has been ripped open wide." With the confidence of a novice, I correctly identified the passive partner in a thousand clandestine perversions.

I became a specialist in the distorted, the twisted, and the bizarre—the loose, tangential thinking characteristic of psychotic process. I learned the language of decay and the spectres of doom that haunted the dreams of the disturbed. Their thoughts of headless animals and worm-eaten leaves portrayed disintegration and disease. I learned to write reports that read like a lawyer's brief documenting disease. Were we trying to justify the bars and locks, the jailer's keys, and the mind-numbing tranquilizing drugs? Or were we so obsessed with labels and the telltale signs of schizophrenia because we had to justify our own existence in the grim, macabre game? Did we ever think of them as people who lived and worked and loved before they lived behind locked doors? It is hard to recall.

I first met Mary Ellen shortly after her admission. A pixie-like blond, she was acutely paranoid, delusional, and belligerent upon arrival. Medication was prescribed, and she was included in a group therapy class. Things went well at first. Mary Ellen did not seem resentful of efforts to help her and was trying to separate her dream world from reality. She had become a polite, cooperative patient. She seemed ready to accept the notion that her religious theories, to which she had so tenaciously clung, were projections of her resentment towards her parents and her needs for affection. Individual psychotherapy was recommended, and I was assigned to see her for this purpose.

Her folder summarized her early history and the events leading up to her breakdown. Born in a dreary coal town in western Pennsylvania, Mary Ellen was a sickly infant. She never really knew her father and later told conflicting stories about him. There were a series of three stepfathers, but none ever cared for her. She had seizures until the age of three. Her family considered her a bright but "odd little girl."

Twelve-year-old Mary Ellen became incestuously involved with her older brother and bore his child. The infant had multiple congenital anomalies and died two months later. Mary Ellen was not allowed to see the child. She finished high school, then made a few false starts at a career. Since nothing seemed to work, she became a WAF. A soldier would have married her, but she could not decide what to do, and he found someone else.

She spent four years with Uncle Sam; then, a

civilian once again, she tried her hand at acting, but found she lacked talent. Returning to her mother's home, she tried some other jobs, but things didn't improve. At business school she found it hard to learn, and pressures started mounting.

At first she blamed her mother, then her friends. She went on buying sprees; she started taking pills to stay awake. She had long spells of crying, smoked incessantly, and would not eat.

She knew there was a master plan; her voices told her what to do. She searched out signs to prove her special mission. She could look directly at the sun and keep her eyes wide open! She met the Archangel Michael.

She read the Bible night and day and evolved her own philosophy. All men were devils, she believed. She would establish an ideal world; the way God wanted it. She had a personal relationship with God and when she prayed, she called Him "Daddy."

Just prior to our first meeting, Mary Ellen had become intoxicated on the ward and was solicited for a homosexual affair with two other female patients. The three were discovered together. Mary Ellen became hysterical when they were found. She said she loved the woman, but had no memory of what she had been doing. She denied sexual desires ("My body is dead from the neck down."), but craved the understanding promised her.

I reassured myself that I could prevent Mary Ellen from complicating her pathology with a homosexual relationship. Such a relationship might force this moralistic, guilt-ridden girl into another psychotic breakdown.

During the first interview, Mary Ellen conveyed a

strong desire to trust someone. She indicated that she was aware of the consequences of becoming a lesbian, but denied any shame about it.

"What do you think makes this relationship so attractive to you?"

"When I was fourteen, a friend of my stepfather lured me down to the cellar. He made me fondle his privates. Since then, I have found sex with men to be disgusting."

"Why didn't you turn to your mother for help?"

"All she cared about was herself. I'm never going home again."

"You seem now to distrust all men."

"A man is incapable of understanding and consideration."

"But have you really found that now?"

"When I first met Liz and Ginny, I was fascinated. They had their own family. Liz was the husband, and Ginny the wife. I asked if I could be the baby. No sex or anything. I just wanted to be loved."

"That didn't last very long."

"Pretty soon the baby grew up and decided she wanted the father, and that's all."

"Earlier you turned to the Bible for help."

"I'm trying to think about what made me get those ideas. It seemed like so many things were backwards in the world. The seven sacraments, for example. The first is baptism and the last is extreme unction. When you die, it is like being born again, so you should get baptized."

"There was a special relationship between you and God."

"I loved Him in a sense different from many men and women. I had a detachment from sex, but I wanted to look nice for Him. He took the place of father, brother, and lover."

"Yes?"

"I invented a game I played with Him. I would purposely mislay something and say that God was hiding things from me. Then I would hide things from Him. I got a kick out of it. I made crowns for the Blessed Mother and Jesus. It was a silly little game. I know it didn't hold any water. I don't know if it was my illness or not."

"You wanted it to be real."

"No. It was just a silly game. But God knew about it. He knows everything. You can't hide from God. I loved God so much that I wanted to do little things for Him as a surprise. I would hide things and say: 'You angels and saints keep God busy.' It was just pretend. Doesn't everybody pretend with his loved ones? Take Christmas gifts and sneak them into the house? I pretended I wanted to remain on earth at all times, even at the end of the world. Who am I to go to heaven? I've sinned."

"Isn't that the crux of the matter?"

"I don't know. I used to think: 'Am I committing a sin by thinking these things?' I must know the reason for these thoughts. I tried to avoid blaspheming. I rarely swear. I formed a habit to say 'Bless it!' rather than 'Damn it!' My mother always swears. People don't stop to think what they are saying. When I'm discharged, I'm going to go to church three or four times a week. I'm going to lead a good life, regardless of what is going on around me. Maybe I'll write to you in a few years and tell you what has happened."

The following day her girlfriend, Liz, was discharged. Within a few hours Mary Ellen had gone AWOL. I heard that they had set up housekeeping together, and both had jobs. Two months later I met Mary Ellen, by chance, at a bar outside the gates. She had returned to see her old friends, she said. They were to smuggle out some medicine for her. "I'm doing fine and very happy. Don't worry about me. It's all for the best."

Perhaps she really did want help but couldn't bring herself to ask. I couldn't persuade her to come back and soon gave up the effort. Later, I heard rumors that Liz and Mary Ellen had separated. One of them had slashed her wrists. I don't know which. Anyway, it didn't work.

I left Perryville shortly after that and have never journeyed back. Perhaps she did return and is there yet, for all I know. Perhaps some other intern is more accepting of her needs, and has special ways of meeting them. For me, there have been other patients—(I call them clients now). But only rarely have I glimpsed again the "Other World" so briefly shared with me.

5

Who's Abnormal?

The seminar was scheduled from 5:30 to 7:30 P.M. each Tuesday. Childhood Psychopathology, as it was titled, covered a broad range of content areas. I was a Visiting Professor, moonlighting after hours. I had organized the fifteen-week semester to deal with neurotic and psychotic disorders, brain damage and learning disabilities, behavior problems, and mental retardation.

The class, which was exceptionally small, was an ideal teaching situation. Five graduate students were enrolled. As a group, they were bright and well motivated. Dottie was aggressive and challenging—a super-sophisticated New Yorker with some resentment toward the program, and problems in taking examinations and presenting material to the group. Jean, a housewife, was too quiet, absorbing everything, taking copious notes, but contributing little to discussions. Charlene, also married, worked as a teacher, and had some clinical sophistication about kids. She was young, just out of college, black, and confused about what to believe. She knew there were opposing theoretical orientations and seemed to be struggling to identify with some position, but with little basis on which to form her allegiances. I knew Barbara from another seminar. She could be relied upon to be supportive, was a conscientious student who read and memorized everything, but needed to learn to develop her own ideas. John, on the other hand, was full of good ideas. He wanted to discuss everything; but, as I found out later, he didn't read assignments. Potentially a good group—students who would respond well to the clinical approach and to the material which would be presented.

I wanted the first seminar to be a good one. I intended to review the historical antecedents of psychopathology, and to define some limits for the content of the seminar. I would pose several questions to the group in the attempt to lead their thinking in certain directions, and then fill in where needed with relevant information. Is there a definable area of study which we can label psychopathology? What are the limits of abnormality? Is the area of child pathology distinguishable from psychopathology in adults? Where do we draw the line about pathology as qualitatively different from normal behavior? How do these concepts relate to earlier concepts derived from religion or superstition? Are the phenomena labeled pathological reliably measured? How can we explain abnormal behavior? Is it learned?

"We are here to learn something about psychopathology in children," I began. "I will try to guide your progress. Since I am more of a professional psychologist than a professional teacher, I am in a position to share my experience with you in working with the kinds of problems we will be reading about. Although a good part of our time will be devoted to discussion and your original thoughts, this cannot be the extent of your involvement. I want you also to become fluent with a body of knowledge. I will direct you towards a series of relevant readings, which I expect you to do. There will be a final examination, which will reflect the readings as well as our class discussions."

I began by presenting a rather extreme position.

"The idea of psychopathology is not new. It was not so long ago that all illness was conceived as psychological. The use of prayer, magic, sacrifice, and exorcism, as treatment for physical disorders, reflects this belief. Even today Christian Scientists, Oral Roberts, and psychosomatic medicine operate under the same assumptions. Some claim that electroconvulsive shock, psychosurgery and drugs, and even psychotherapies, are not far removed from witchcraft."

"Aren't you stretching a point to draw parallels between witchcraft and psychotherapy?" Dottie asked. "After all, we have made some scientific progress in understanding human personality dynamics."

"I'm not so sure about that. I am not arguing the point about the effectiveness of psychotherapy here, although the evidence that psychotherapy works is scanty. But witchdoctors may be equally effective. It is only western man who labels their efforts as magic and unscientific—'Witchdoctor' is our label, not theirs. In their own societies, they are accepted as professional healers, just as favorably as psychologists and psychiatrists are accepted here. Perhaps better."

"Accepted, yes. But surely you're not saying that their mumbo jumbo has any validity."

"A psychiatrist named Torrey has made a study of

the counterparts of psychotherapists in more primitive cultures. He finds the same four components found in western psychotherapies are also found in primitive witchcraft. The first he labels the 'Principle of Rumpelstiltskin,' or "putting a label on the conditions." It is very reassuring for people to know what is wrong with them. It doesn't matter much whether we call it schizophrenia, or say that the spirit of an ancestor, whom we have offended, inhabits our body. The other three components are the personal qualities of the therapist, the expectation that he can help, and the specific techniques of therapy, which are not as different as you might believe."

"I've always felt that psychotherapy was quackery."

"You miss the point. There is nothing unique about psychotherapy. Even behavior therapies have their counterparts in some cultures. Torrey tells us that in Western Nigeria an acceptable method of toilet training a male child is to tie a toad to his penis. When the boy wets, the toad wakes up and croaks. This also wakes the boy up, and he learns to inhibit his wetting. If any of you are familiar with the enuresis conditioning pads in common use in this country, you will recognize the same principle. So, psychological explanations of pathology are not a new idea and are not unique to western cultures. How about the reverse side of the coin? What have you read about the concept of a natural origin of mental disorders? Barbara, help us out here."

"Everything always goes back to Greek philosophy, so I guess Socrates, Plato, and Aristotle had something to say about that. I can't remember what, but I know Hippocrates saw hysteria as a feminine disease. Misplaced womb, or something."

"Yes, his cure was to anchor it firmly back in place by 'lighting the torch of Hymen.' He also disputed the popular notion of epilepsy as a 'sacred disease' and defined natural factors as causative agents. Go on."

"Galen was the Roman philosopher who developed a theory of 'humors.'"

"Bile, phlegm, blood, and gall."

"They accounted for fluctuations in temperament. We still call people phlegmatic."

"You have a lot of gall pointing that out."

"That idea is not very different from modern conceptions of the effects of hormones upon emotions."

"Now you're thinking. O.K., you're off the hook."

"What about witch burning during the Inquisition?" Charlene interjected.

"It was a regression. The witch was thought to be sexually promiscuous. Have you ever heard of *Malleus Maleficarum*, the Witches' Hammer? This was the authoritative textbook of the Inquisition on the identification and punishment of witches. It was written during the 15th century by Heinrich Kramer and James Sprenger. I found some quotes from it in a paperback, written by Jan Ehrenwald. Listen. 'What, then, are the evil things witches, in cooperation with the devil, can bring about? They range from the practice of black magic to corrupting man's mind so as to betray his Christian faith. They may cause illness, mental and physical. And they may, above all, entice man to indulge in all sorts of sexual deviations. The witches themselves are the chief perpetrators of such crimes; they copulate with devils and other demons and are capable of begetting children with them. In any case, the root of the evil lies in man's carnal desires, or, anatomically speaking, in his, or her, 'privy parts'.'"

"Compare that with Freud's sexual etiology of the neuroses, and the psychoanalytic view of unconscious determinants of behavior."

"I can bring us up through the Renaissance and the nineteenth century."

"Go ahead, John. Glad to know you're still with us."

"The hold of religious dogma upon medical practitioners was broken. A humanitarian movement took hold. This paved the way for Pinel to release the deranged from their cells. The 'alienists' at the Bicetre in Paris had a more scientific interest in the natural causes of mental illness. Mesmer and Charcot began experimenting with hypnotism as a treatment method, and this led eventually to the work with hysterics of Janet, and later Freud."

"O.K., you've done your reading. But do you see the trap that got us into?"

"I don't follow."

"The abuses that existed in treating the mentally ill and mentally deficient, described in this country so elegantly by Dorothea Dix, led to an overreaction in the opposite direction. It was more humanitarian to treat hysterias, obsessions and psychoses as illness rather than as the work of demons, or evidence of sin. But there was no real evidence for a physical basis of mental illness either. The end result of all that reform was to put mental disorder squarely in the medical bag, and to ignore social and environmental determinants. The medical model of mental disorders, which is being so strongly challenged by behaviorists and social psychiatrists today, had its origins with Pinel and Dorothea Dix."

I tried to pull things together and push the discussion further.

"Well, then. We have traced the development of

both the psychic and natural explanations of mental illness, and you can see the historical threads. But, how far have we really come today? In what ways do we define pathology in our society?"

"One way is statistically," Jean volunteered, "but I know that is not enough."

"You'd better explain."

"We tend to think of normal in terms of the frequency of its occurrence. Something that happens often is acceptable to us. If it is rare, we may not accept it. The term 'abnormal' implies deviation from the mean, but has assumed more negative connotations."

"You seem to disagree with that."

"Because a behavior is infrequent should not, necessarily, make it pathological. Low intelligence is abnormal in a statistical sense, but so is high intelligence. We don't diagnose mental retardation on the basis of a low IQ, but because the retarded person cannot cope in school or on the job."

"Yes. Then you are suggesting another criterion for judging pathology—one that relates to adaptiveness of the behavior in question. If a behavior has adaptive value in our society, and if it helps us cope with demands, it is considered healthy or normal. If a behavior is maladaptive, it is unhealthy."

"That's all so cold and objective," John chimed in. "What about more humanistic considerations?"

"Such as?"

"Happiness, satisfaction, feelings of self-worth, depression, anxiety. You know what I'm talking about."

"Those things are less visible to others, but they certainly seem equally important. They are sometimes lumped together and called 'criteria of adjustment.' I tend to think of them as the input, or cost, at which we adapt to environmental demands."

"Wait a minute. You're all being very smug about

defining who's abnormal. Just because someone doesn't fit in well with what society considers normal, you want to put a label on him. I don't think anyone can come up with a criterion of abnormality or normality. What is normal in one society is abnormal in another."

"O.K., John. You're attacking the concept of a universal dimension of pathology. I disagree with you, but go ahead and make your point."

"Anthropologists have described many behaviors in other cultures which we would consider bizarre, but which are perfectly acceptable in their own settings. An Alaskan chief may communicate with his ancestors. This is part of being a chief. If you transported him to Philadelphia, and he did the same thing, he'd wind up in a state hospital. There is an example where the same behavior is socially acceptable in Alaska, but is labeled delusional or 'crazy' here. It's all relative."

"That sounds like a legitimate criticism of the whole concept of psychopathology. Can anyone offer a rebuttal?"

"I don't think the two situations really are all that similar."

"Explain, Charlene."

"The delusions of the Alaskan chief are perfectly adaptive to his tribe. In fact, they are strongly determined by the social values of his culture. They don't tell us anything about the personality of the chief. The delusions of a schizophrenic, on the other hand, may be the only way she can solve some internal conflict. A paranoid female, who believes all men are out to rape her, is projecting her own instinctual impulses outward, impulses that are so threatening to her whole system of values that she cannot recognize them as her own. So, even though the delusional behavior seems similar in the two cases, one is pathological, the other is not."

"That's pretty heavy, Charlene, but I couldn't agree more. If we keep our point of reference within the individual, then the issue of cultural relativism seems spurious. Will you yield, John?"

"No, it's too pat. The projection mechanism in your illustration is just our attempt to understand the delusion. The environmental pull on such behavior may be just as strong in the schizophrenic as the Alaskan chief. And labeling such behavior as 'sick' doesn't allow us to deal with it any better. It may do more harm than good."

"O.K., but now you are attacking what we do after we identify abnormal behavior. If it is the medical model you are unhappy with, you're in good company. We will get to that at a later date. Let's stick to definitions of abnormality today."

"I don't see how you can separate the two, but I'll let you go on."

"Jean, you've been pretty quiet. Do you have anything to add to this discussion?"

"I am not happy with definitions of abnormality. It's all so negative. If we could agree upon what is normal or healthy, there'd be no argument about what is abnormal."

"Good point. What did you have in mind?"

"Humanistic psychology makes a lot of sense to me. I think Maslow was on the right track. He defined psychological health in terms of the gratification of needs. Once the basic physiological needs are satisfied, psychological adjustment is determined by the satisfaction of more complex needs, like esteem, belongingness, and love. He said the highest need is to develop oneself to the highest potential and to be able to care for others in a truly selfless manner."

"That sounds like religion, not psychology."

"He called it self-actualization, John, and it does

have a religious. significance. How many people really attain that level of development? I have a quote to illustrate Maslow's point. 'Let us say that person A has lived for several weeks in a dangerous jungle, in which he has managed to stay alive by finding occasional food and water. Person B not only stays alive but also has a rifle and a hidden cave with a closeable entrance. Person C has all of these and has more men with him as well. Person D has the food, the gun, the allies, the cave, and in addition, has with him his best loved friend. Finally, person E, in the same jungle, has all of these, and in addition, is the well-respected leader of his band. For the sake of brevity we may call these men, respectively, the merely surviving, the safe, the belonging, the loved, and the respected. . . . But this is not only a series of increasing need gratification; it is as well a series of increasing degrees of psychological health.'"

The seminar ended well. We had raised more questions than we had answered, but the students were interested. I had paved the way for future discussions. The year ahead looked bright.

6

Alice in Rorschachland

The year of internship was dragging. Clinical training was interesting, but the workday ended at five, and within ten minutes, the last of the long line of cars had filed past the gate. The long grey evenings hung heavy, and I needed something to occupy my time.

My dissertation sat within a box high on a shelf, waiting to be rewritten for publication. I made a few abortive attempts, but the task became aversive. Instead I found a new diversion.

Rorschach evaluation was a skill recently acquired. The Veterans Administration patients provided a continuous flow of pathological responses so grotesque that they seemed to reflect a Wonderland gone wild. I tried to express my growing involvement with the technique by means of a satirical fantasy, which had gradually captured my imagination. Spouting innuendoes decipherable only by Rorschach devotees, Alice would grope her way through the ten Rorschach inkblots. Despite my enthusiasm, the story was left half finished when I returned to Philadelphia a year later to my first professional job.

Ten years had slipped by when Jerry, our compulsive housekeeper, threatened to burn the contents of my desk if I didn't do something about cleaning it out.

Hiding crumpled behind the center drawer was the handwritten Rorschach parody. I had all but forgotten the forced puns. I laughed at my own stumbling efforts at humor. I spent a week finishing it and, tongue-in-cheek, mailed it off to a very staid journal editor who took assessment more seriously than I had obviously done ten years ago.

Within a month the acceptance arrived.

"We would like to print your amusing paper," the editor explained, "but would you kindly forward a hundred word abstract to comply with the journal policy."

"He has a sense of humor, too," I reluctantly acknowledged. "But how could Alice be abstracted?"

"Why, of course. It's not the technique that deserves my ridicule. Who, besides Alice, can fault a pack of cards. It's the misuse of the procedure that I found humorous." In good conscience then, I wrote the hundred words explaining:

"Misconceptions and misuse of the Rorschach technique are parodied in this Alice in Wonderland story. Alice falls down a rabbit hole and journeys through the Rorschach Plates until she is tried at an Inquiry on Card X. The story can be interpreted as critical of Rorschach practitioners who search only for pathology, not health; ignore the free associative instructions to the client; and restructure reality along Rorschach dimensions of personality and terminology."

I

Alice was beginning to get very tired of sitting with her sister on the bank and having nothing to do. She was considering in her "mind" (she always considered her mind in quotation marks) whether the pleasure of making a daisy chain would be worth the trouble of getting up and picking the daisies, when, suddenly, a green rabbit with curvy eyelashes ran close by her. There was nothing very remarkable in that, nor did Alice think it so much out of the way to hear the rabbit say to himself: "Oh, dear! Twenty minutes late. I shall be contaminated." When she thought it over afterwards, it occurred to her that she ought to have wondered, but at the time, it did not seem at all bizarre. But when the rabbit actually took a stopwatch out of its waistcoat pocket and looked at it and then hurried on, Alice started to her feet. It flashed across her "mind" that she had never before seen a green rabbit with either a waistcoat pocket or a stopwatch to take out of it. Burning with curiosity, she ran across the field after it, and was just in time to see it pop down a large rabbit hole under the hedge.

In another moment, down went Alice after it, never once considering the problem of size constancy. Down, down, down. "Will the fall never come to an end?" she said aloud. Or at least she thought that she said it. But she was falling faster than the speed of sound, so she couldn't hear if she had said it or not, and since there was no one else around to hear (the green rabbit had long since vanished), she really couldn't be sure.

Down, down, down she fell, quite sorry by now that she had jumped so impulsively without evidence of either appropriate ego control or proper judgmental processes; when thump! thump! thump!, she landed upon a heap of sticks and dry leaves (at least they were shaped that way, but were clearly the wrong color), and the fall was over.

Alice was not a bit hurt and jumped up on her feet in a moment. She looked up to see nothing but blank space over her head. All around her was a black dreary expanse, sometimes broken by varying shades of grey or white, but not a speckle of color. She was just contemplating the possibilities of an organic basis for her perceptual distortion (she had given her cortex quite a jar in the landing), when all at once the green rabbit reappeared. There was not a moment to be lost. Away went Alice after him and was just in time to see the rabbit turn a corner (I would describe the corner, dear reader, but since it is only a rare detail, I will not tarry here), and to hear him exclaim: "Oh, my ears and whiskers, how late it's getting. I must get to X before the Inquiry," and off he ran and was soon no longer to be seen. All at once, Alice, who was now beginning to remember how lonely she was and how nice it would be to be sitting by the fire with her cat, Dinah, began to cry.

"Mustn't cry, you know!" she heard, and looking up, realized that she was sitting at the feet of a great Halloween mask (or at least what would be the feet of a Halloween mask if Halloween masks had feet). "How strange!" thought Alice, "but then everything today is strange."

"What kind of a bird are you?" asked the strange-looking mask. By this time Alice had looked closely and could make out two eyes, a nose, and a mouth.

"I'm not a bird at all. I'm a child," replied Alice indignantly.

"A human child?" asked the mask.

"Of course," answered Alice, by this time summing up enough courage to answer the mask directly.

"Impossible! Only one human on this card, and she has no head."

"Well, I have a head," said Alice, "which is about all that you have, I believe."

"Don't be impertinent," said the mask. "You're being scored, you know."

By this time Alice was so confused she didn't answer at all.

"Why were you crying?" asked the mask. "It's the black, you know," he continued without even waiting for an answer. "Makes us all a bit down in the mouth."

"Everything is so queer today," explained Alice.

"Queer?" questioned the mask, suspiciously.

"Yes. I'm sure I'm not the same girl I was yesterday."

"Write that down," said the mask (to no one at all that Alice could see). "And remind me to bring it up at the Inquiry."

"I'm certain I must have changed," said Alice. "I'll try and say 'How doth the little'." She crossed her hands on her lap, as if she were saying her lessons, and began to recite. But her voice sounded hoarse and strange, and the words did not come out the same as they used to.

> How doth the little butterfly
> Remember who he wuz
> Before he learned to question why
> When he wuz only fuzz?
>
> Is he the same short wiggly worm
> Or is he any more for this,
> When he politely takes his turn
> At completing metamorphosis?
>
> And likewise what remains with us
> When we are twelve or thirty,
> Of thoughts and feelings long ago
> When we were small and dirty?

"I'm sure those are not the right words," said Alice, and her eyes filled with tears once again.

"Certainly not," said the mask. "No matter. Go find the March Bears on Card II and ask them to tell you their story."

"March Bears? What, pray tell, is a March Bear?"

"Dunce! You're obviously of borderline intelligence. You've heard the story of the Emperor's New Clothes, haven't you?"

"Oh, yes. He paraded naked in front of his subjects, but I don't see what that has to do with it."

"He Marched Bare, didn't he?"

"I never thought of it that way before," replied Alice.

At that the mask began to grow fuzzier and dimmer. Its edges slowly ran into the white background until all that was left was a huge grinning mouth . . . and then it disappeared.

II

"Curiouser and curiouser," thought Alice. "A moment ago I was talking to a mask, and now here I am seated between two black bears playing pat-a-cake. "Pease porridge hot," shouted the First. "Pease porridge cold," cried the Second, even louder. Before they could get to the nine days old part, Alice interrupted.

"Finally, something I understand. May I join in?"

"No room," said the bears in unison.

"Nonsense," said Alice. "There's plenty of room."

"In what way are an orange and a banana alike?" asked one of the bears.

"Oh goodie, riddles," said Alice, always eager to demonstrate her skill with abstract material. "They're both fruit."

"Wrong!" cried the First Bear. "They're not alike at all. One's round and orange, and the other's long and yellow."

"Failure to discriminate," replied the Second Bear. "Write that down."

"Oh, stuff and nonsense," said Alice, not one to be easily put down. "Oranges and bananas are both fruits, as well as apples and grapes and peaches and pears and pomegranates."

"Word salad," said the First Bear. "Pathognomonic," added the Second.

"I think you're both horrid," Alice thought, but not wishing to appear impolite, she ignored the last remark. "The mask said to ask you to tell your story."

The March Bears sighed deeply and began to sing in voices choked with sobs:

You've seen bears in the circus and bears in the zoo,
But we are the bears who live on Card II.
We play pease porridge hot, we play pease porridge
    cold.
If you don't see our movement, you're not very old.
If we look like two bunnies, don't spread it about,
If you see us in color, you're really freaked out.
Do you see us up close, do you see us from far?
Are we soft? Are we fuzzy? Do we shine like a star?
Are we two dimensions, or do we have vista?
Are we lady or man bears? That's our business, sister!
Do you see us dressed up in red hats and pink vests?
Do you see us as friendly? Do you think we are pests?
Do you think we are skinny or maybe too fat?
Just what do you think has made you say that?
The shape of our paws or the form of our noses,
Do you really know what deep problems this poses?
Do we look like Russia, or maybe the Tsar?
You'd better lie down girl. You're really bizarre.

"I'm sure I didn't understand a thing you said," commented Alice.

"Naturally," said the First Bear. "We knew it right from the start. Your thinking is confused. You're probably disoriented in all three spheres."

"I may be disoriented," returned Alice, "but at least

I'm not bleeding."

"I knew it! I knew it!" said the Second Bear. "She sees blood."

"Shocking," added the First Bear.

"Fiddlesticks," said Alice, ignoring their disdainful glances. "Your paws are bleeding. You really should wear shoes, you know. Wait! I think I have a Band-aid in my pocketbook. I'll have you fixed up in no time at all."

As Alice tried to apply the Band-aid to the First Bear's foot, the bears recoiled in horror.

"Stop it! Stop it!" they screamed. "She's creating a color disturbance. Call the Examiner!"

"I knew she'd use that medical model sooner or later," said the First Bear. "Get her," he growled.

At this the two bears bared their fangs and leaped at Alice. It was only at the very last second that Alice noticed the spinning top way off in the distance—a large white twirling top that made a strange humming sound as it approached—"m. . .m. . .m. . .m. . ." In a moment, the top was upon them. It twirled right in between the two bears and, just as the bears were about to pounce on Alice, she leaped onto the top, grabbed the center post with both hands, and held on tightly. In another moment, the top and Alice had left the bears far behind, and she heard them resume their pat-a-cake game.

III

The top zigged this way and that, and once Alice was far enough away from Card II that the bears could not reach her, she began to relax and enjoy the scenery. This was a strange country she was travelling through. It had trees and grass and animals and people, but everything and everybody was of two colors—some a shade of greyish-black, and some a variant of reddish-pink. At first Alice was somewhat taken aback by the lack of variety, but after a while, she hardly noticed, and everything began to seem quite natural to her. Soon, the top slowed down enough so that Alice could jump off without falling. She started to walk down a beautiful garden path when, turning a bend, she encountered two strange looking cannibals. They were dancing round and round a large pot shaped like a pepper. They looked so much alike they must have been twins. Above the pot hovered a monstrous red butterfly. The cannibals were stark naked except for a high tight collar of pearls they wore around their necks. The strangest thing about the cannibals was that sometimes they looked like women, and sometimes they looked like men. The more Alice looked, the harder it was for her to decide just what they were.

Although Alice was beginning to feel very hungry (it was at least an hour beyond the time when Nanny served her afternoon cookies and milk), the pot did not smell at all appetizing. The cannibals were pouring far too much pepper into the pot, so much so that the red butterfly, who was hovering too close to the pot for comfort, was continually sneezing.

"What are you cooking?" asked Alice, hoping to make friends, although at this point she really couldn't be sure that the cannibals might not want to place her in the pot.

"Why, pepper pot soup, of course," the cannibal twins replied in unison.

"And why do you put so much pepper in it?" asked Alice, innocently.

"We ask the questions around here," shouted the cannibals. "What are you doing here anyway?"

"I'm sure I don't know," answered Alice, now beginning to feel somewhat unwanted. "I was riding the spinning top, and before I could say *Psychodiagnostik*, here I was." (Alice sometimes spoke in German when she wanted to impress, and although she hadn't the slightest idea of what *Psychodiagnostik* meant, she was sure that neither did the cannibals.)

"Well," answered the cannibals, "you are very lucky to be in our company on this card. We're very popular, you know."

"No, I don't know, and what's more, I really don't care. I think you're very rude. And what's more, you still haven't told me why you cook with so much pepper."

At this, the cannibals resumed their dancing and began to chant:

> Speak harshly to your butterfly
> and eat him when he sneezes.
> He's introverted and he's shy,
> and when it's cold he freezes.
> If you see butterflies, it's good.
> Your passions do not rule ya.
> But if you see more than you should,
> then brother, you're peculiar.

While they were singing, the cannibals began to dance around the pepper pot. As Alice watched, they seemed to be changing in front of her eyes from men to women, and back to men again. Faster and faster they turned until they seemed no more than a flash of light.

"What are they doing?" she asked the Red Butterfly, who still hovered between them.

"It's their Liberation Movement," explained the Butterfly. "It all started last week when they began arguing whether it was better to be a man or a woman. They couldn't decide so they keep changing back and forth. It's a kind of metamorphosis, I think. Would you like to join their Movement?"

"Certainly not," Alice responded indignantly. "I'm perfectly happy being just a girl. Besides, they change so often I can't tell what they are, and I'll bet they can't either."

At that, a pair of grotesque red monkeys swung down from the trees under which Alice happened to be standing and began jabbering at her so rapidly that it came out a jumble of words.

"Sexual confusion," one Swinging Monkey accused, over and over.

"Projection," shouted the other, again and again.

Louder and louder they shouted, swinging by their tails closer and closer to Alice, and pointing their red paws at her face. In a short time, their words became so confused that it seemed to sound like "Profusion" and "Sexection" and "Pro-con" and "Conjectual", all mixed up in a melange of noise.

"Quiet," screamed Alice, when she could stand it no longer. "I can't hear myself think!"

"Why would you want to do that?" queried the Butterfly. "Suppose you listened and didn't hear anything. Better leave well enough alone."

"It's just an expression," answered Alice, as she tried to recall the last time she heard herself think.

"Well, it sounds pretty silly to me," said the Butterfly. "I think what you probably meant was that it was so noisy you couldn't think yourself here, and then you wouldn't be, of course."

"Wouldn't be what?" asked Alice, growing more and more confused.

"Be where, not what," corrected the Butterfly. "Your grammar leaves a great deal to be desired, you know."

"Beware of what?" screamed Alice, by now very much annoyed.

"Of Godzilla, of course," answered the Butterfly as he slowly began to melt.

Now Alice had seen butter melt many times, but

she couldn't recall ever having seen a butterfly melt before, but things were so strange today she didn't even question it.

"Before you go, won't you please tell me how to get to Card IV?" asked Alice, politely.

"I really haven't the authority," said the Butterfly, or at least what was left of him.

"Please," implored Alice, "I can't tolerate this noise one more second without reacting violently."

"Just take the Approach you've been following. It's only a little bit farther," said the Butterfly's antennae, which was all that was now left of him.

Alice took his advice and before long she was confronted with Godzilla on Card IV.

IV to IX

Alice continued her journey encountering many strange and wonderful creatures. On Card IV, she met Godzilla—a monster ape who rode on top of a sacred cow, named Hermann, and did his best to scare Alice by trying to squash her with his Italian boots. Alice narrowly escaped when Godzilla's arms turned into long-necked geese, who advised her to crawl through the Monster's cave to Card V where Godzilla had no authority.

On Card V, Alice ate the magic grass and began to shrink until she was no bigger than Projection—the Winged Bat who asked how he affected her. When she looked closely at the Bat, he turned into the Green Rabbit, who had now turned grey and black.

"How shocking," he responded, when Alice asked how he changed his color.

The Rabbit told Alice that she was obviously depressed and cautioned her to inform the Examiner of this when she arrived at Card X.

"That's mad," Alice answered angrily.

"We are all mad, here," the Rabbit informed her, and hurried off so as not to miss the Queen's Inquiry.

Suddenly, Alice encountered two ferocious Crocodiles—Oral and Sadistic—who chased her off their Card.

When Alice got to Card VI, she was very tired. Ahead of her, she saw an immense foxskin rug. It looked so inviting she curled up on it and went to sleep. When she awoke, she found she had attained her full size. "How nice and warm and soft and shady it is here," she thought out loud.

"Infantile! Infantile!" shouted the Foxhead.

"I'm only a little girl, you know," returned Alice.

"No matter," answered the Fox, "your social development is immature."

"Imagine that," said Alice.

"That goes without saying," said the Fox. "Now leave at once. I no longer wish to associate with you."

"I'm leaving," snapped Alice fulfillingly, but the Foxhead never heard her. In a moment, he dissolved into a large fluffy cloud shaped like the letter K, and Alice knew instinctively she had arrived on Card VII.

Alice walked around the entire outline of the K, keeping both feet on the fuzzy grey border, being careful not to step off the edge and fall into the white space that existed all around. This was difficult since the outline kept changing and shifting until Alice grew quite dizzy, and just a wee bit anxious. Just when things looked like they couldn't get any worse, they did. Alice met the two Indian Squaws—Tweedle Do and Tweedle Don't. They were perpetually battling. Tweedle Do always wanted to have fun. "I will," she cried. Tweedle Don't always saw the negative side of things. "Better not," she warned. Tweedle Do and Tweedle Don't invited Alice to a C party on Card VIII. "What's a C party?" Alice asked innocently.

"Why don't you come and C?" replied the Indian Squaws.

"I think you are both horrid," responded Alice. "I think this whole place is horrid. Everyone tries to see what's wrong with me. No one ever tries to see what's right with me."

"She's quite mad, you know," Tweedle Do remarked.

"Darn right I'm mad—so mad I could scream."

"Better not," said Tweedle Don't.

"See you at the party," interrupted Tweedle Do, ignoring both remarks. "Don't forget to wear your colors."

The C party wasn't a party at all, but more like a race. Everyone had to find a partner and race up a tall mountain. When Alice arrived, the March Bears were climbing neck and neck to the top.

"What do they do when they reach the top?" Alice asked.

"Come down again, of course," answered the two Orange Dogs, waiting their turn at the bottom. "You really are simple," they added. "Where's your twin, anyway?"

"I have no twin," replied Alice,"only a big sister who's still sitting on the bank by the rabbit hole, where I wish I was now, if you must know."

"For shame!" said the First Dog. "Everyone here has a twin. We're all symmetrical. That's the way we keep our balance. Why, if there were no twins, the Card would become unbalanced, and we'd all fall off into the white."

"It's a very high climb," continued Alice, who by this time had learned to ignore things she didn't understand, which was almost everything that was said to her these days.

"Persevere," said the Dog.

"What's that?" asked Alice, who was only in the second grade and knew that severe meant hard (like the Pilgrims having a severe first winter in the New World), but had no idea what "persevere" meant, although she guessed it might be a hard purr like Dinah, her cat, made when he purred in his sleep.

"Never mind," said the Second Dog. "You'll perseverate naturally. We all do here sooner or later. Go find your twin. No use staying here. You can't play without a partner. Besides, you're the wrong color. You clash, and you'll ruin our color balance."

"Your what?" asked Alice. "Oh, never mind. You'll just say more nonsense. I'm leaving."

And she did.

On Card IX, Alice encountered the Orange Witch riding on the horns of the Green Moose. The witch invited Alice to a game of croquet to be played on top of a pink cloud. When Alice protested that the cloud would not support her, the witch accused her of lacking stability, and asked her to respond to a riddle.

"If a table is stable, when is an untable, unstable?"

"Let's table the issue," Alice answered, punningly.

Just then the Green Rabbit ran by, and, removing his stopwatch from his waistcoat pocket, announced excitedly:

"You'll be late for the Queen's Inquiry. Hurry! Hurry! You must get to Card X for the Inquiry."

Everyone rushed to Card X, and Alice was drawn along with the mob.

On Card X, Alice observed a bizarre underwater ballet in which crabs and frogs and sea horses of varying sizes and colors contorted in grotesque gyrations. The Queen was an enormous blue octopus with soft, spongy legs constantly wiggling in a menacing manner toward Alice. It screamed throughout the entire proceedings:

"Off with her red! Off with her red!" presumably referring to the scarlet red ribbon Alice wore to tie back her hair.

Finally, the Examiner, who was apparently both Judge and Prosecutor in the case, called the Court to order, and Alice began to realize that it was she who was on trial. Alice was made to account for her earlier remarks under penalty of Miss Diagnosis, the Court Bailiff.

"Answer the Whole Truth and nothing but the Truth," cautioned the Examiner, "including even the most insignificant Details. Remember, we are all here to help you."

I'll try," replied Alice, "although I can't possibly see how any of this will help me."

"What is your location?" asked the Examiner.

"I live at 823 Orchard Lane," replied Alice. "It's the first house on the left side of the street, the one with green shutters."

"Your card!" the Examiner persisted.

"Well, I've been to all of them," Alice said indignantly, "but I certainly wouldn't want to live on any of them. They're not even nice places to visit, I'm sorry to say, let alone to fall into through a rabbit hole."

At that, the Green Rabbit gasped and turned a bright purple, sputtering and coughing uncontrollably.

"Off with her red!" shouted the Queen.

"Order! Order in the Court!" shouted the Examiner, writing furiously on his yellow tablet. "We must get everything down in the proper sequence."

"You told the Halloween Mask on Card I that you

were not the same girl you were yesterday, I believe. What was it that made you say that?"

"Are you the same as you were yesterday?" countered Alice, "or aren't we all changed constantly by the multitude of experiences and sensations that we encounter each moment?"

Alice was quite proud of that response and sat back smugly in her seat, beginning to enjoy the proceedings somewhat.

"Try to answer the questions, please," the Examiner responded reproachfully. "What I want to know is, what is it about the Card that made you respond as you did?"

"I'm sure I can't determine that," persisted Alice, forming her words carefully. "And let me remind you that according to law, I'm innocent until proven guilty, and free to associate with anyone I please."

"Not here," retorted the Examiner, momentarily losing his objectivity. "It's guilt by association at this Inquiry."

"Off with her red!" screamed the Queen.

"Stuff and nonsense!" Alice shouted back at her. "I understand it now. It's nothing but a silly game with its own crazy rules. Only nobody wins."

"She's hysterical," screamed the Queen. "Write that down!"

"How do you score it?" asked the Brown Crayfish, who was apparently the Court Recorder.

"I'm leaving," said Alice, and she began to walk off the witness stand.

"You can't leave," shouted the Examiner. "I've only just begun my Inquiry."

At this, an angry cry arose from the spectators in the gallery.

"Off with her red!" demanded the Queen, and

lifted her eight tentacles to snatch at Alice's hair ribbon.

"You can't help me," returned Alice, immediately. "You're nothing but a pack of cards, and not very useful ones at that. You're certainly not much good for playing War and Old Maid and Go Fish."

At this, there arose a general furor amongst the jurors, and all of the Cards flew at Alice. She screamed and fell over backwards, hitting her head against a grey stovepipe that two hideous Frogs were trying to hold in the air and climb at the same time. The last thing she saw before she fainted was the grinning face of the Green Rabbit, whose eyelashes had turned into two Green Seahorses.

The End

7

The Girl Who Told Stories

Jean was eighteen, and a freshman at the University. A bright, aloof girl, she dressed in a manner reminiscent of her Greenwich Village background. Her long, straight hair and disdain for make-up afforded her a "beat" appearance in the days before this was fashionable. The slight stoop in her gait and rounding of her shoulders revealed her self-consciousness about her height. Jean was anxious and depressed. She was seeing a psychiatrist at the University Student Health Office.

Jean's Rorschach imagery consisted of long, leggy females (like herself), cuddly animals, brightly colored flowers, thinly veiled seductive references, and blatantly erotic and aggressive responses.

From the Rorschach protocol, I speculated about a hysterical and narcissistic girl who acts out her emotional needs with insufficient planning and inadequate judgment. Jean needs to be admired. She trades on her sexuality, seeking warmth from men, but finds only sexual encounters. Anxious because of basic insecurities about her self-worth, she looks to men to prove that she is adequate. But sex is not her basic need, so

63

she responds aggressively, and never satisfied, she winds up guilty and depressed. Like the spider in her Rorschach, Jean views herself as an ugly bug. With only sex to offer, she must be sexual.

Narcissism and depression are two sides of a bad coin. Jean needs to flaunt her legs and hair and lips at men to prove she is a woman. Invariably she finds no one can satisfy a bottomless affectual pit; she is perpetually unfulfilled.

Unlike the inkblot test, the TAT shows real people in real situations. "Thematic Apperception" is a fancy name for telling stories. The method was developed thirty years ago for assessing personality needs and environmental pressures from the subject's point of view.

"Just tell a story to each picture. Use your imagination. Describe what might be going on, and what led up to what you see, and how it all turns out. Don't forget to mention what the people there are thinking or feeling."

The story teller projects into each production a little of himself. Deprive him of his lunch, and he will tell of food. Show nude slides at his fraternity house, and he'll give sexual references galore. Jean continues to describe herself:

"This is a little lonely boy, and he has lived in a dark garret all his life. His mother has to work all day; and he is blind. She comes home at night with little interesting things from the big house at the top of the hill where she works. Things for him to play with and to amuse him during the long, hard day. One day, from the top of the hill, she gets an old violin that was given to her that was in the attic. She was pleased to bring it home to her son so he could learn to play. Well, he practiced for a while and couldn't learn to read notes, and right now is desperate about the situation and has given up all hope. He'll put it away in the corner and sort of plunk it every now and then."

*   *   *

"Oh, my. This is a very interesting story. Mary, who is a high school girl whose parents have died, lives on the farm with her older sister and her husband. The older sister is pregnant. Now, the marriage is an unhappy one. Mary's older sister is very much in love with her husband, but her husband is not in love with her. He's in love with Mary. He's kind of a coarse fellow, and Mary's sister is really very bright. She fell in love with him originally 'cause of physical attraction. But they're pretty incompatible. Mary doesn't know how to handle her feelings, which are pretty ambivalent. She has feeling for her older sister, but is in love with the man. What will happen finally is that Mary, realizing that there is no future in ruining her sister's life and her own because of all the guilt feelings she has, decides to leave the farm and go to the city and get a job."

*   *   *

"This is a story of a girl who is born in Canada. She goes to New York to go to Barnard. She already is about three-fourths through with school. She has been to some big university in Montreal, when she was in Canada. So she gets a little apartment on 116th Street, and she goes to school and works at night, and she's very much alone. She gravitates to the Village and meets various unhealthy people who have lots of their own problems. She becomes aware of people and their problems. She was originally naive. She finds herself drinking and sinking in many respects. She meets a

man at a party and is very attracted to him. She's not a
good looking girl, and he isn't very interested in her.
She becomes obsessed with the idea of marrying him.
He's good for nothing, a Village Bum. But they become
friendly. He thinks he can derive something from the
relationship, a free meal maybe. The relationship becomes involved, she emotionally; not he. One day he
meets someone else and leaves her, and she cracks up,
sort of, and ends up in the psychiatrist's office where
she is right now. She undergoes protracted therapy; and
she'll go back to school at Columbia—Barnard—and
she'll fall into a similar pattern again; and she'll go back
to the psychiatrist, and this will continue. She will
finish school and get a job, and finally it will be recommended that she go back to Canada. She will, and she'll
teach in Canada and devote all her energies to this, and
she'll never get married or become socially active. She
will lead a very lonely life with all her energy devoted to
her teaching."

*   *   *

"This takes place in Havana, and it's about an
American architect who meets a Spanish girl from one
of the best families, and they are in sophisticated,
aristocratic circles. They wine and dine together
(spoken sarcastically) all the time and they become
engaged. But he gets a message from home that his
parents don't approve, and he writes them a heated
letter about how much he loves the girl and is going to
marry her. But the problem is he has an inheritance
coming up, and it's threatened to be cut off. Being
selfish, he weighs the situation over and decides to
leave the girl. But he really loves her in his own way,
and she doesn't want to lose him; so they run away

together—without getting married—for a few months, and nothing is heard of them. He knows he has to be back in the United States by the first of the year, and when the time rolls around, he leaves her for good and returns home."

*   *   *

"This is Aunt Martha—the unmarried sister of Mrs. Society Bug. But she is about twenty years older than Mrs. Society Bug and is pretty much around home all the time, while the family goes about its business. The children regard her as an odd bug, and the husband doesn't pay much attention to her. Nor does her sister for that matter. She is a very self-conscious person, but is very polite and kind and generous, but very, very mild. She is afraid of interrupting others and doesn't consider herself as anyone of importance. She'll live in this house till her death, which won't be very long because she has some kind of disease which will kill her relatively early."

*   *   *

"This takes place in 1922, let's say, and the woman in the picture is a young lady in her early twenties who has graduated college—one of the few in those days—but is rather wild in the sense that she hasn't settled down to get a job. She lives in the city in her own apartment where she parties and goes on skiing trips and has one good time most of the time. She is one of the feminists—for voting and drinking and smoking for women and has cut off her hair and is an intellectual. At the present, she's having an affair with the fellow with the pipe in his hand, but that will soon be over, and she'll meet a nice businessman who falls in love with

her and marries her. She becomes very conventional
and happy, and, except for minor problems we all have,
she lives happily—quote—forever after."

*   *   *

"This is the story of a little refugee, who is left an
orphan, at approximately two years of age, during the
war. She was brought up to about the age of five in a
convent without love or affection of any kind. She
grows up a little, hostile, bitter child. When she's six,
however, some relatives in the United States get word
of her existence and have her sent over here, where she
is adopted by a second cousin. The mother, or step-
mother, tries very hard to make up for all the time she's
lost; but unfortunately, there are deep-seated hostili-
ties in the girl which cannot be overcome by dolls and
superficial sweetness. The child is friendless because of
her foreign accent and her hostility toward other
children. But her adopted mother is very patient and
very kind to the child and tries to give her love and
understanding. Do I have to continue out the lives of
these people? (Any way you wish.) The child will
superficially become integrated with the other children;
but will grow up unhappy, very sensitive, and marred
by her early experiences."

*   *   *

"It's so obvious now. This woman is modeling for a
painting by a modern artist. She is an artist herself, and
she poses for her husband, and he does the same for
her. They are very happy, but poor, except for one
thing. She shows more promise than he does; but he's
making more money than she at the present time, so
his jealousy is minimized because he does realize she
has more potential than he. One day someone sees her

work—a great critic. They arrange for someone to commission some work to do. She's coming to the fore. He's accepted her greater talent and has overcome his earlier immaturity. One day she is crossing the street and is run over by a truck and killed."

*   *   *

"I'm not sure I understand this picture. This story is about a houseparty in the country near the beach in which there is a whole crowd of people. They all know the host, but they do not all know each other; and they meet this weekend. They are all intelligent people and really settle down to interesting things—reading seminars in the library; outside they have various sport classes; in the evenings they have cocktails; and they talk and sit down to continental-type dinner at 8:30 P.M.—all very pseudosophisticated, but really enjoying themselves. They haven't come up as couples. However, one girl sets her eyes on a fellow, and she decides that he's pretty much it; but there are a lot of attractive women there. She doesn't know very much about him, but is attracted to him, and watches him carefully. She finally wangles sitting next to him for dinner, and everything she's thought is doubly confirmed; but he doesn't say anything about after dinner, and he disappears. She follows him and hides behind a tree on the beach where he's walking back and forth and finally sits on a big rock. A girl comes running out. They meet and sit and talk, and obviously they quarrel, and he strangles her and throws her in the water. The lady behind the tree is shocked and runs back to the house not knowing what to do; yet, she can't keep away from the man, and the next morning they play tennis and eat lunch and go to the garden. The murder of the previous night seems like a nightmare, and she erases it out of her mind. Well, time passes, and they go out, and come back from the houseparty, and see each other constantly. Two or three months later they are invited to another houseparty. One evening, after dinner, he says that he is going for a walk and would she meet him later on the beach. She does. They talk and quarrel, and he kills her."

*   *   *

"This is a couple from Czechoslovakia, who are very unhappy under the political situation. The husband has the opportunity of getting out of the country now—if he can manage to make it to the border—and get to France where he has important connections; then, he'll be able to arrange for her and the children to leave also. So they weigh their decision for a period of two weeks or so, and, finally, it's time for him to try to escape. So, right before he leaves, they say goodbye to each other, hoping that everything works out, and he leaves at five o'clock in the morning. She waits a week, two weeks for some sign—a month, two months, and she becomes more nervous and excited. However, she can't talk about it to anyone. After six months, she's sure he's dead, and it begins to affect her mind. She's unable to concentrate on things and is no longer a responsible person as far as her children are concerned and, after a year, has a nervous breakdown and is taken to the hospital. On the day she is taken to the hospital, a message comes from her husband that he had been captured and escaped and is now safe in France, but the message was written in code, which they had arranged beforehand. When the message was taken in by one of the children, it was thought of as a joke and thrown away."

*   *   *

"This is a picture of a castle in which a princess has been charmed by a dragon who loves her very much. But she is horror-stricken by the dragon and would rather stay shut up in a castle than have anything to do with him. But, since the dragon loves her so much, he does nice things for her—brings her cakes and wines and entertains her with magic. She almost becomes happy except that she has no companionship. She begs the dragon to let her go home to her father, but he can't let her go. So, finally, he decides, because he loves her so much, he'll let her go see them, but they can't see her. So, she's allowed to be transported home. To her dismay, she finds the castle a shambles and her father and brothers gone. She returns sadly to the home of the dragon. She's so upset that she consents to stay with the dragon forever."

*   *   *

"This is the country, and this boat has been left alone for a long time by some fisherman. But it's in use by the children from the village nearby, who come and use it to go up and down the stream or little lake, as it may be. They usually catch frogs and go fishing from the boat. One day about six of them come up for a fishing expedition. In the excitement the boat over-turns, and they all grab for it. They are good swimmers, but the boat gets broken and pieces just float around, and the boys have to swim back to shore without doing any fishing."

*   *   *

"Hmm. The woman in the picture is a dope addict. The man is her husband. He is in the army. He doesn't leave her with very much money. She has two very young children, but she's stupid and always under the influence of some dope. She also drinks too much, but her husband doesn't see or know very much of this and is away so much of the time. But one night he returns home unexpectedly and finds her on the floor in a drunken stupor, and the children are screaming in the next room, and the gas is on. The pilot light has gone off, and he can't believe it's his own house. He picks her up and puts her in bed and wipes his brow and thinks about what he's done wrong. At first he's angry with his wife and blames her for her situation. But then he realizes how she's been alone and how he never considered her problems. He'll leave the army as soon as he can get a job and see if he can't make something of their marriage and help her.

*   *   *

The hysterical character is one in whom affective life and emotional reactivity prevail as a life style. Jean seems to combine such traits with a narcissistic orientation to people and to circumstances. Her image as a feminine seductress is important to her, since she sees this as the avenue by which one obtains life's gratification. She needs to be alluring. She needs to be the victor in her encounters with males more than likely as a repetition of her lifelong experiences with the first important male in her life, her father. Jean must be able to tell herself, "I am beautiful, adequate, and competent," especially in feminine characteristics and pursuits. To accomplish this end requires a defensive structure designed to deny feelings of inadequacy. But, Jean walks a narrow path. Her defenses have crumbled to some extent. A feeling of inadequacy, a fatal flaw, and a damaged self-concept threaten everything. She is no longer able to deny her depression, and her behavior becomes so blatantly seductive that even she must be aware of its underlying purpose.

We can speculate that these dynamics have made Jean unhappy at home. She provides us with clues that she is somewhat like her mother—a Bohemian rebel against convention and society. Mother, herself a narcissist, is too involved with her own problems to understand Jean. And how about father? Is he the prototype of the brutal, coarse, unfeeling, and rejecting male whom Jean repeatedly seeks out and loses? We can guess that the repetitious compulsion for unsatisfactory heterosexual relationships, which Jean seeks, is a perpetual re-enactment of the relationship with her father. Like the situation at home, her failure at romance confirms her basic incompetence and reinforces her sense of guilt. No matter how she rebels, Jean seems destined to feel unworthy.

These stories have no end. Perhaps Jean found help for her problems from the psychiatrist she saw. I never learned, and it all happened long ago.

8

Just a Nervous Habit

The scientist watched the child fondle the white rabbit. "Nice rabbit," the assistant cooed as she stroked its fur. Tentatively, the eleven-month old mimicked her actions. With growing confidence, Albert braved playing with the animal. At last he smiled his approval. "Good, warm, soft rabbit," he thought. "Touch rabbit."

Stealthily, the assistant advanced behind his back. In her hand was a large iron bar. Unseen by the child, she crept as close as she dared while still avoiding detection. Raising a small steel hammer to the bar, she gave it a sure, swift blast. Albert jerked first in disbelief, then terror. Dropping the rabbit from his lap, he crawled away in panic, wailing loudly in full retreat.

Each day Albert returned to the laboratory. Each day the assistant tried to approach with the rabbit. But each day Albert screamed at the first sight of the animal, and struggled to escape. A piece of wool, a fur coat, and a Santa Claus mask produced the same response. Carefully, the scientist noted each struggle, each whimper, and was pleased.

Freud had explained fears as nothing more than anxiety "bound" to some object. It's not the fear that needs treating but the anxiety beneath. The failure of repression, or the return of the repressed to consciousness, that's what constitutes the crux of the neurosis.

"Not so," the scientist reasoned. "Fears are simply learned. Associations are the answer. A twist of fate may pair some object or event with something that is painful until that object, itself, elicits fear. Why, Albert may grow up with rabbit phobia and never recollect our sessions in this lab. And, if he should consult some neo-Freudian for treatment of this neurotic trait, he could spend five years on the couch in search of submerged impulses to masturbate or other bedroom trauma; but he'd search in vain. It was Pavlov who supplied the key, not Freud."

And the scientist wrote it down in books, and called it "Behaviorism."

In 1924, another psychologist, another child. This child had already learned rabbit fear. The psychiatrist wants to cure him of this phobia. Psychoanalysis? No.

The child sits at a small table helping himself to the lunch. Kid-type food like peanut butter and jelly sandwiches, potato chips, and chocolate milk. Ice cream for dessert. At the far end of the room stands the experimenter, a rabbit in her arms. The child looks up apprehensively, but the rabbit is far away. He continues eating. Gradually, not too fast, or food may become aversive, the rabbit is brought closer.

"Have another bite of that sandwich, child. Yummy, isn't it?"

She brings the rabbit a little closer. Still later, the child sits and strokes the rabbit. No signs of fear. Nice rabbit.

Nice demonstration. Treat fears as habits; responses conditioned to specific stimuli. If fears are only that, we should know what to do. Whatever's learned can be unlearned. Psychologists know the rules.

The library's filled with studies of how Norwegian rats, dogs, sows, cockroaches, and earthworms learn. Sure, humans are more complicated, but the principles of learning are the same, and drive and cue and reinforcement have all been well explained. Why not treat behavior in the human animal as well? That a child was cured of rabbit fears was scientifically recorded, and every first year psychology student can quote the journal reference. But few psychologists did therapy, and analysts still talked of underlying conflicts and repression.

Bedwetting can humiliate a child and destroy the image that he has about himself. When he goes to summer camp for instance, and sees his sheet hung out to dry with a telltale stain in the center, it becomes his yellow badge of shame.

"Anxiety," said the therapists. "Play therapy is required to find what really troubles him." "Bad habits," said some others, and while the Panzer troops were sweeping across Europe, they built a simple apparatus that stopped a child from wetting. The enuretic must be made to feel the pressure of his bladder no matter how deeply he sleeps or dreams, or what his level of anxiety. A piece of muslin placed between two metallic sheets can do the job. The sheets are wired to a battery and bell and perforated so that when the child wets, it soaks down through the holes and the muslin becomes a conductor. Each night the alarm is set, and the stain grows smaller as the child awakens sooner. And, if it works, he will awaken before the bell when pressure from his bladder becomes the stimulus for waking up. Today, the method is accepted, and you can buy an enuresis pad at Sears.

In the fifties things perked up a bit. Two psychologists at Yale translated much of Freud's concoctions into terms that were more palatable to those who studied rats. Anxiety and conflict, displacement and repression all found their counterparts, and psychologists were happy. But, it still didn't change the psychotherapists much.

A scientist at Harvard was teaching rats to press a bar and pigeons to peck at lights. And, he designed a box in which to bring up infants. He also thought of ways for teaching children, step-by-step, by methods classroom teachers never used. He wrote a book about a world where reinforcements were scientifically dispensed, and some people tried it. His students said, "Let's do these things with those people where mother nature's been a bitch and programmed poorly; or where society has run amuck and built abominations called mental hospitals, or jails, or schools for mentally retarded."

Behaviorism started in Canada, then in Illinois. The behaviors that we label sick or crazy need not be that way at all. A young psychologist irritated some; but the hospital director was convinced that he was right and let him try.

The patients were "far gone" and sat around or lay around on floors. Some would not eat unless they were dragged to meals and fed by spoon. A few required intravenous feeding. The psychologist built a door that opened automatically when meals were served; then locked again. Each day the time of the opening of the door was shortened just a bit so that the patients had to rush to exit before the lock clicked shut again. And soon the door wasn't open very long at all, and a dozen chronically withdrawn and vegetative souls were rushing through.

He placed a subway turnstile before the dining room, and as each hungry patient came for lunch, a friendly nurse slipped a token in his hand. It was the entrance ticket. When everyone had learned the way to gain a meal, the system changed. They had to ask a nurse if she would give them the token so they might eat. Some patients rarely spoke at all. But when they wanted food inside their guts, they spoke.

Once tokens became valuable, they could be used to reinforce whatever was appropriate, like working at a hospital job, or dressing neatly, or reading a newspaper, or talking about what bothered them. The tokens bought them weekend passes, movies on Friday nights, and a private room with a TV. The hospital economy was based upon the tokens, and it was found that hearing voices, talking crazy, and belligerence decreased in frequency when all the reinforcements came for other ways of doing things. Administrators had to think about the ways their hospitals perpetuated sick behavior, such as giving tender loving care for what is inappropriate and weird. And, doctors had to think a second time about whether "voices from the radiator" were signs of schizophrenia. Or, were they merely things that people learned to do when other patterns no longer worked and hallucinations were useful substitutes?

A South African psychiatrist became impressed with American Behaviorism and, being far removed from prevailing spheres of influence, did some thinking on his own. He schemed about a way to deal with the neuroses by teaching behavior incompatible with anxiety and fear. Relaxation was a response that could be used as therapy. One can't be scared and calm at the same time, so why not teach neurotics to relax when they are tense or fearful. The idea wasn't new, but he gave it some theoretical sophistication, and it caught on. He found a way to use imagination to make the world less frightening. Teach relaxation first, then have the patient fantasize, in gradual steps, whatever makes him tense. The crazy thing was that it worked for phobias and obsessions. So he explored some other behaviors, antagonistic to anxiety, like assertion and sexual response. He did experiments with cats to prove his point.

Graduate students read his book and designed scientific studies with control groups. Patients were found who jumped when they saw snakes, or could not fall asleep at night, or trembled when they had to talk in front of groups. Results with the new technique were better than with the old talking method, or with no therapy at all, and a generation of psychologists nodded their approval and climbed aboard. All the answers weren't there, and later, rapprochements were made between the old and new; but in the early days when therapy was stagnated by neo neo neos trying to outdo each other by splitting hairs a little finer, it was a cool, refreshing wind.

Times, they were a-changing. But I was young and in a clinic where the establishment was strong.

"Lady Macbeth" was almost sixty, her hair was white. A tired-out Irish widow wasn't of much interest to the psychiatric residents in training, or to their prosperous analytic supervisors with gold chains across affluent bellies.

"Let the new psychologist see her. He needs the experience; but supervise him closely."

She washed her hands and arms until the skin was raw and bleeding. Like a whirlwind, she descended on my office and ran right to the sink and washed, pulling the paper towels off the dispenser and flinging them on the floor. She had to leave her house and take the trolley, touching filthy coins and brushing against the riff-raff. She had to turn knobs and handles and infect herself with all the clinic germs, and so she had to wash.

Poor Lady Macbeth. Her house was a mess because she spent her time scrubbing her hands. Filth accumulated on her carpets and her draperies, and she couldn't bear to touch it.

For fifteen years she'd been a widow. She lived with Joe, her strapping son, who was now eighteen and interested in girls. Joe was staying out late in dives with no time left for his mother.

It was the drug she'd taken, she angrily accused. Her symptoms had begun because her heart medicine had been polluted by the druggist, and now she'd caught some horrible plague which made her wash her hands.

But, I'd read Freud, and I knew differently, and my supervisor agreed. The day before, she spied her son bending over the garden fence and picking up something from the ground, then tossing it carelessly away. For some reason she was curious, and later, she walked over by the fence to examine what he'd seen. She picked up the dirty rubber condom and thought a lot about it afterwards.

Her son was muscular. He loaded freight at Sears. Sometimes, when he came home all tired and sweaty, she would rub his back. She'd been a widow fifteen years, and she was lonely.

On the inkblot test she became upset.

"Those cards are messes," she insisted. "Just dirty spots and stains. I can't see anything."

She was hard of hearing, and she asked me to repeat every word I said to her. You see, the hearing aid was never working right, or the batteries were dead. But when she wanted to, she heard.

We talked for hours, and she explained how lonely she had been and how neglectful children were, what a terrible effort it was to ride the trolley car, and couldn't I provide her, please, with some miraculous medicine to stop her awful washing. I tried hard to be supportive and to never say how angry she must feel, or how guilty.

At last I left the clinic to follow other gods, and Lady Macbeth was transferred to the doctor she had wanted from the start, the one who gave out medicine. Perhaps she rubs her hands today. Perhaps she still comes for her weekly chat with some new young psychologist. But no, she'd be too old to engender much interest. Her symptoms are "old hat," and who can hope to change what is so well entrenched? Perhaps I might have helped her at the time, if I had tried the newer heresy. But, it was much too soon.

9

Tomorrow You'll Be Glad

Jackie was almost three and still wasn't toilet trained. We had done everything—praise, rewards, consistent routines on the toilet; but she was much too stubborn. "Reward even minor successes," the books had said, but you can't reward something that doesn't happen.

"How will I send her to nursery school?" Bonnie moaned.

"Strap a pottie to her behind," I advised.

She went to nursery school all right, and never had an accident. But she never used the toilet either. Just held it in all morning and flooded when she got home. We wrapped a rubber pad around her mattress, but that didn't keep the sheets dry, or her pajamas, or the blankets, or her damned teddy bear.

"We'll get you big girl panties," her grandmother promised, "with pretty embroidery and ruffles."

Jackie was not impressed. Her quarter-inch thick training pants did nicely, thank you. For years grandmother had been nagging us to get her toilet trained.

"You were trained at eight months," she pointed out to Bonnie, "and Jackie's already past two and still wetting herself. You ought to be ashamed. And a psychologist's daughter, too."

But, we were going to be relaxed and train her when she was ready.

"People just don't do the things you did in your day, Mom. Lots less hassle this way, you know. Just relax about it, will you?"

So we relaxed and so did Jackie. Somehow, we had never gotten around to training her, and now we had to do something. I set a chart high on the bathroom wall, and every time she tried, a bright red star was pasted in a box. And, animal crackers were stored within the medicine chest. If she went, I wanted her to be rewarded fast. Each hour she would sit for ten minutes, no more, and soon the chart was filled with stars, but not once did she oblige. But, after getting up from that accursed pot, she'd slink off to some corner and there would be a flood.

At last my wife had had enough of stars and cookies and soaking pants, and me and my psychology. Determined now that she'd succeed, she took things in her own hands. The thing she took was Jackie's bottom and gave her one resounding smack each time she wet. The shot heard 'round the world had nothing on that blast. I gritted my teeth in disapproval but, having no alternative, sat back and let matters take their course.

For Jackie, things were clear. She had to yield or to suffer for it. She could not wet her pants for fear of punishment; she'd have to try it our way.

Not yet, she didn't. Instead, she vowed she'd keep it in—and in—and in—ad infinitum. Six hours she held, then eight, then ten. We watched her with concern. For how much more could sphincters hold in assiduous defiance. Twelve hours went by, and still she sat and let out not a drop. Her eyeballs were turning yellow!

In panic we called up Doctor Dave.

"Dave, tell us quick, how long can children wait before their bladders burst?"

"Stick with it. You're almost there," he reassured. "Tomorrow you'll be glad."

At last she sat down on the seat and let it all come out. And, that was it. No more upsets, no more smacks, and lots of big girl panties.

Two weeks went by, and sure enough, a client had a child who was almost four and refused to use the toilet.

"Let's do it quick," I urged. "One smack each time she wets or soils. Just make sure she gets up on the pot once every hour, and lots of fuss for each success."

"Dr. Rosen, are you sure? She's gone twelve hours and still won't go."

"Relax," I said. "You're almost home. Tomorrow you'll be glad."

10
A Shocking Episode

When I first saw Danny, he was the center of a minor holocaust. I was Chief Psychologist at a large residential school for the mentally retarded. I had been asked to visit his dormitory to see if anything could be done to control his biting. I couldn't have arrived at a better moment.

Danny was being held in the vise-like grip of an obviously distraught houseparent. A chubby child was screaming hysterically, his hand gingerly caressing an angry red mark on his arm. Teethmarks were plainly visible. On seeing me enter the building, the houseparent lost all vestiges of control.

"They should pull out all his teeth," she screamed. "He's like an animal."

A ring of children took in the scene, and picking up her hysteria tauntingly parroted back, "Pull out his teeth."

Danny was thirteen years old and had lived at the school for two years. Without language and with severe behavioral disturbance, he was a constant management problem to houseparents and teachers. His diagnosis was Chronic Brain Syndrome, but his emotional problems were so severe that he might also have been labeled autistic. He related poorly to adults, often seeming to look right through another person without establishing eye contact. He had many stereotyped motor gestures, such as twirling, and was hyperactive and distractible. His dexterity and motor coordination, however, were excellent. Danny was a handsome dark-haired boy and, were it not for his behavior, could be mistaken for normal.

I have two mementos of my contacts with Danny, both of which I hope never to use again. The first is a three-foot-long cattle prod, the kind used by certain sheriffs in Selma, Alabama, during the black demonstrations a decade ago. Using 7 D-cell batteries, it provides quite a jolt when the handle is depressed and the two electrodes are held firmly to the skin. The other is also a shocking device, less offensive to the sensibilities, but equally painful. Specially made for us, it was attached to the leg by an ace bandage and activated by a remote control unit from a Zenith TV set. The second device allowed us to shock Danny from a distance of a few feet without drawing undue attention to what we were doing.

The use of punishment to discipline or control behavior is a controversial procedure. It raises many questions of ethics. There is no question that it can be a powerful suppressor of behavior. The efficiency of totalitarian methods of control provides ample evidence that punishment, or the threat of punishment, can produce marked changes in behavior. Electric shock has been used to control self-mutilative behavior among the severely retarded, when such behavior threatens their life. However, it is difficult to administer punishment in a controlled fashion. Many parents punish in anger, and it is sometimes difficult to determine when punishment becomes cruel or sadistic.

Ivar Lovaas has used aversive conditioning, within

the context of a great deal of positive reinforcement, in his work with autistic children at the Neuropsychiatric Institute at UCLA. He suggests three possible uses for aversive conditioning. The simplest is the punishment for an inappropriate behavior by following it immediately with a slap or electric shock. The second is the reinforcement of an appropriate behavior by terminating a punishment when the appropriate behavior occurs. The third involves the pairing of a previously neutral stimulus with the avoidance of shock in order to increase the value of that stimulus to the child. Lovaas has attempted to teach greater affective involvement of autistic children with their parents by allowing them to run to their parents in order to avoid shock.

There was evidence that Danny had been punished while at a psychiatric hospital where he was a patient prior to coming to the school. The admitting physician had indicated that he should not be placed in isolation, since he would become very disturbed. Reportedly, on such occasions, Danny tore his clothing, threw food, and bit his own arms. Although we reluctantly followed this directive, we had ample opportunity to witness the same behaviors when he was not in isolation.

The summer we began working with Danny, his biting of other students became quite severe. The building supervisors and teachers were having trouble controlling this behavior, and were finding it difficult to protect other students. His bites were deep and drew blood. He usually selected rather passive, non-aggressive children for his attacks so that he met with little resistance. While he sometimes misjudged and bit a child who fought back, he seldom made the same mistake twice. There was considerable pressure from parents of other students to "do something" about Daniel.

Daniel's biting seemed unprovoked, only insofar as

the behavior of his target was concerned. But our observations suggested that the response was more frequent when Daniel was jealous of the attention other students were receiving. If a teacher's attention in the classroom was directed at Daniel, his behavior was usually appropriate. Should she turn her back, however, to deal with another student, the chances were high that he would strike out.

Whatever the motivation, it was obvious that the biting was an attention-getter for Daniel. The general result was usually pandemonium. Biting provided Daniel with a great deal of individual attention throughout the day. Whether in school or in his residence building, Daniel was frequently controlled by someone holding his hand in order to prevent his biting. Even this was not always successful. Physically adroit and fast, Daniel was sometimes able to squirm away and inflict his damage well before his chaperone could react to stop him.

The power of attention is often underestimated. When there are two or more children in a family, each child quickly learns to compete for parental attention. When as many as twenty children are separated from their families and placed under the charge of one or two houseparents, their attention-getting maneuvers may become extreme. If a child finds a way to elicit more attention, even in the form of reprimands and punishment, he will learn to use this method. We believed that it was attention that provided the primary mechanism for Daniel's biting.

The situation had deteriorated rapidly. He was biting many times a day. Houseparent staff were generally negative about him and were pressuring for his discharge. There was a general attitude of fear and anger harbored by those with direct responsibility for his care. Recommendations by staff to "muzzle" him were sometimes made openly in his presence. Many of the more passive children were visibly afraid of him. Daniel's name was brought up repeatedly in weekly staff meetings, and the handwriting was on the wall. Daniel would soon be discharged because of his dangerous and disruptive behavior. We agreed to help, although we knew we might be fighting a losing battle.

Sensitive to the reinforcing properties of attention Daniel was receiving, we hoped to find a way of removing the attention he received for biting by providing attention only for appropriate behavior. Three college students were employed to work with Daniel. Our idea was to provide him with individual attention during all his waking hours, but to ignore him after every bite. The three students would alternate, working in three shifts, beginning at the time Daniel awakened in the morning and lasting until he went to bed at night. The students were taught to keep records of the frequency of daily biting, and were trained in applying principles of reinforcement.

We held a series of in-service training meetings with the staff of Daniel's residence building. The basis for the program and what the students were instructed to do was explained to them. Despite these meetings, the staff remained antagonistic. They tended to see the college student's role as that of a guardian, holding Daniel's hand as they had done, to prevent him from biting. When Daniel did bite, they tended to blame the students for their negligence.

Despite this resistance, the regime seemed to be having some effect. During the four weeks of this reinforcement regime, the frequency of bites decreased from an average of twenty bites each week prior to the program, to thirteen bites each week during the fourth week. However, our program time was running out, and thirteen bites was still a large number. With more time and greater understanding of what we were trying to do, the program might have worked. Continued staff pressure was exerted to discharge Daniel because he was still biting despite the special program and staff. We needed to institute more drastic measures.

Permission was obtained from Daniel's parents and the school administrators to institute a program of aversive conditioning. A remote control shock apparatus was constructed for this purpose. A small shocker, the size of a cigarette package, was secured to Daniel's leg using an ace bandage. The shocker was activated by a TV remote control unit. The apparatus would work from a distance of about four or five feet, and was powered by a transistor battery.

The decision to use aversive stimulation in modifying behavior was not an easy one to make. First, we could not be sure it would work. Second, the prospect of shocking a young child is not a pleasant one. However, all other alternatives had been exhausted.

Daniel was already enrolled in what was probably one of the best educational programs for this type of child that could be found. We knew that discharge was imminent and that he would likely be placed at a state school or home with poor or no educational program. Despite the severity of his behavior, Daniel seemed to understand a great deal. His biting had outfoxed an entire staff of teachers and houseparents. No one believed that the biting was random or accidental. Perhaps the reason he had aroused so much antagonism from the staff was that he was considered devious. Daniel, like many other children with autistic behaviors, appeared to have potential that he was not using.

Once the decision to use shock was made and the necessary permission obtained, we were faced with the reality of actually doing it. None of us was particularly happy with the prospect of applying electric shock to a thirteen-year-old child, even a child with a severe behavior disorder. I have heard other psychologists who have used aversive conditioning indicate that the shock is not really painful, but is merely a strong vibration. Motivated by my own guilt about using shock on Daniel, I frequently felt compelled to demonstrate to people that shock was harmless by applying it to my own hand. These experiences were extremely unpleasant. I would never, in my right mind, apply electric shock to myself for fun.

Initially, the procedure required that someone accompany Daniel throughout the day in order to administer shock after each bite. During the first week of aversive conditioning, biting decreased to ten bites a week. However, the program required a great deal of time to administer. Unfortunately, we were not sufficiently confident of the houseparent staff to allow them to administer the shock. Applied across the heart, the current was sufficient to cause fibrillation and cardiac arrest. The procedure had to be applied by someone who could be relied on.

Daniel was in an open program that encompassed several classrooms, recreational areas, including a swimming pool, dining rooms, and dormitory. A number of different staff members were in contact with him each day. There were just too many people involved and too large an area to cover. We had to find a way of cutting down the staff time needed to control Daniel.

One possibility was to shock him for biting at some time after the incident. The effectiveness of a reinforcement procedure varies directly with the immediacy of the reinforcement. By attempting to reduce the time spent monitoring Daniel's behavior, we also risked attentuating the effects of the procedure. We needed to work out a compromise between immediate reinforcement and realistic time considerations.

As a compromise, we decided to provide Daniel with a secondary negative reinforcement after each bite and to administer the shock at a later, more convenient time. Teachers and houseparents were supplied with Magic Marker crayons and were instructed to draw a single line on Daniel's arm after he bit another child. We arranged to visit Daniel two or three times each day and to shock him on each mark and then erase it with soap and water. If he had two marks on his arm, we were to shock him twice. Prior to initiating the new regime, we had to teach Daniel the equivalence between the mark and the shock—that we were still able to shock him for every bite, but with a delay in reinforcement. Hopefully, the mark would assume some negative meaning to Daniel and would bridge the gap between his biting and the shock.

The initial response to the new procedure was better than we had anticipated. Daniel's biting decreased to only two incidents during the first week of the Magic Marker procedure (the ninth week of our involvement with Daniel). During all this time, Daniel was attending special education classes and recreational programs, so that attempts at teaching appropriate self-help and language behavior were on-going. It was our hope to sufficiently control the disruptive behavior so that Daniel might gain full benefit from the educational effort that was being applied.

Between the tenth and fifteenth week of the

program, Daniel's biting showed a gradual increment. The shock was still being applied but seemed to be losing its effectiveness in controlling the biting. There was even some indication that the procedure had developed some qualities of positive reinforcement. Daniel seemed to be forming a positive relationship with me, despite the fact that I was shocking him!

The shock was still an aversive procedure; Daniel usually resisted strongly when I approached. Nevertheless, we were again providing Daniel with attention when we shocked him. The act of washing off the mark required some time and effort, and Daniel seemed to enjoy that part of the procedure. On several occasions Daniel bit another child, then pulled the houseparent to the telephone, knowing that she would call me to shock him. Apparently, the few minutes of contact were enough to compensate for the pain of the shock. There can be no more powerful demonstration of the importance of attention within the institutional setting.

Daniel's biting was still below the level it had reached prior to the conditioning program. However, it was gradually increasing, and we were growing concerned about the outcome of our efforts. In order to gain a better understanding of what the shock procedure was contributing to Daniel's behavior, we decided to temporarily discontinue the program. On the first day without marks or shock, Daniel bit thirty-four times, almost twice the base rate frequency obtained before we started shocking him. There were eighteen bites the second day. Daniel regressed to soiling, smearing feces, and tearing his clothes. He became more withdrawn and seemed to avoid any sign of recognition of the psychologists who had been working with him. Although he couldn't tell us in words, Daniel seemed to be communicating very clearly that he missed the shock regime! We reinstituted the Magic Marker-shock procedure on the third day after terminating it.

By the twentieth week of the program, his biting had again decreased to three bites a week. But again, the shock began losing its effectiveness. Between the twenty-first and twenty-ninth weeks, biting showed a gradual increase and was varying between ten and fifteen bites per week. During the twenty-ninth week, he experienced several environmental changes in his classroom and living situations. Although the changes were planned to best meet his needs, Daniel showed a serious regression in behavior. He was back to the level of biting he had demonstrated before we began to work with him. He seemed unable to respond to the shock, and the program was terminated. Because of the serious management problems Daniel was presenting, it was no longer possible to maintain him at the Institute, and arrangements were made for transfer to another facility. We had failed.

Daniel was placed in a small residence for the mentally retarded operated by a man and his wife. The home was a large farm-like setting, and there were only five or six other mentally retarded residents. The farm house was in marked contrast to the large, open dormitory where he had lived at our school. In this smaller setting, with less stimulation and fewer demands, Daniel made a somewhat better adjustment. He never began biting at the home. Unfortunately, it was not possible to provide him with educational programming. After a year, an attempt was made to have Daniel attend a Trainable Class at the local school, but his behavior was so disruptive that it was not continued after the first week. Daniel still lives at the farm home, which may be a lifelong placement for him. I hear from his parents every Christmas. He seems happy at the home, but has not gained in intellectual level although he is now almost twenty years old.

When psychologists are successful in their treatment programs, they are usually prone to point to the factors which determined their success. It is seldom that therapeutic failures are printed in psychological texts or journals, so there is little opportunity to profit from the mistakes of others. Yet failures are a very important source of information. Our experience with Daniel taught us a great deal. It is extremely unlikely that I would ever attempt the same treatment with another child unless there was the opportunity for imposing a great deal more control than was possible with Daniel.

First of all, the shock was not the powerful variable we had anticipated it to be. Shock served to suppress the biting somewhat rather than to permanently do away with it. The high frequency of biting when shock was suspended (to a level three times the base rate), was a clear indication that conditioning had not occurred. Daniel inhibited his biting because of the threat of shock. He never learned or became motivated to stop biting altogether.

The failure was ours, not Daniel's. We made the mistake of dealing exclusively with the biting behavior while leaving the teaching of appropriate behavior to others. We failed to teach suitable alternative behaviors. As long as Daniel remained within the same residential situation, competing for attention with large numbers of other handicapped children, we had never really changed the contingencies of reinforcement. When the threat of a severe electric shock was present, he inhibited the biting. When the threat was less immediate, he returned to his old, well-learned habits of gaining attention.

We tried too hard to impose a strict reinforcement contingency, ignoring the opportunity to develop a meaningful relationship. Naively, we wanted the shock to be aversive and tried hard to use it to prevent the biting, which happened despite our efforts. The punisher was still a person to Daniel, and his attention was important. In the interests of maintaining a rigidly scientific experimental climate, we overlooked the obvious. Daniel's therapy required a person who could impose the aversive stimulation when it was required, but also one who could provide positive social reinforcement in the form of a relationship and who would, in addition, be the teacher of important social behaviors. Perhaps with this kind of regime, negative reinforcement would never be required.

In order to have been successful with Daniel, we needed a small controlled environment for imposing training regimes. It was an almost impossible task to train the many teachers, houseparents, and recreators with whom Daniel had daily contact. Daniel needed the structure and consistency of people who would be with him every day and who were trained to be consistent in their treatment. An intensive treatment unit where Daniel could live and attend school was needed, but such a facility was not available. Within such a unit, it would have been possible to provide specialized treatment programs for several students, rather than to expend the time and effort on only one child. Such units do exist in certain psychiatric settings, but they are rare, costly, and generally unavailable to children like Daniel.

11

The Middle Finger Caper

Jeff was not a child one could easily forget. I was asked to see him because of his unmanageable and seemingly incorrigible classroom behavior. I had arranged to meet him in the Education Center, using the school psychologist's office for this purpose.

He was already waiting when I arrived. His flaming red hair and freckled face gave him an air of twelve-year-old innocence somewhere between that of Howdy Doody and Harold Teen. First impressions are often misleading. In this case, they were completely unnerving.

"I'm Dr. Rosen," I explained, in my most friendly professional manner.

"I'm not going to stay here," Jeff announced, "and you can't make me." At that he bolted from the room and ran down the corridor, daring me to give chase. "Ran" is not really an accurate description of his behavior. Actually, he twirled with great agility, keeping me always in sight, and emphasizing his disdain by repeated gestures with the middle finger of his right hand, and tongue protrusions in my direction. His occasional four-letter profanities barked at no one in

particular were especially upsetting to the very
proper school principal scowling at Jeff and me from
behind her desk.

In 1885, Gilles de la Tourette described a "nervous
affliction" characterized by repetitive and compulsive
shouting of obscene words. The condition typically
begins in childhood with tics which progress to involve
the upper limbs, trunk, or the entire body. Later, vocal
tics develop, such as frequent coughing, clearing the
throat, or grunting. Finally, the obscenities begin.
Although patients have been known to be relatively
free of symptoms for months or even years, the condition is resistant to all forms of treatment.

Some authors believe an organic disturbance of the
brain underlies the symptoms. A few sufferers
deteriorate intellectually in later years. However, solid
neurological support for this theory is lacking. Other
theories attribute the symptom to psychological factors. Certainly the early family life of such children is
replete with difficulties. But, again, after reviewing the
available evidence, one group of investigators concluded that psychological factors are unrelated to the
cause, useless for the diagnosis, and irrelevant to the
treatment of Tourette's syndrome.

Jeff was living in a special unit at the school,
designed for emotionally disturbed children. A psychiatrist worked with the staff and helped to structure a
therapeutic milieu. The staff had learned to tolerate
Jeff's twirling and profanities. Oh, there were times
when it got out of hand, like during the Sunday services
when Jeff made a travesty of a solemn mass. They
didn't feel he needed exposure to religious experiences
after that. But gradually, Jeff was accepted within the
residential unit. It was in school where pandemonium
broke loose.

A classroom of disturbed children is never a picnic for a teacher. It's one thing to recognize that a child has emotional problems, and that things are not so good at home, if there is a home. It's something else again to try to teach a bunch of loud, aggressive, angry, frightened, rebellious, intimidated, defiant, and sometimes destructive, kids to form their letters cursively, or to add a row of numerals. Mrs. Williams just wasn't prepared for Jeff.

Jeff's troubles seem to have begun around the time he started school. He was hyperactive, or so they concluded. He sucked his thumb, made barking sounds, and jerked his head spastically. His father was a martinet, but punishment only made things worse. The parents were advised that a special therapeutic day school would help Jeff. Well, he didn't last long there. He started breaking things, and his barking sounds gave way to gutter words. He was soon being transferred from one residential institution to another.

His EEG was normal; no signs of organicity. He had average ability, and IQ tests were old friends. He'd taken them so often. Yet, questions that he did not know upset him more than usual. He asked how other boys had done.

All through the testing, which I administered, he shouted words I knew he always used. He seemed to be watching me for a sign that I was unnerved or angry with him. I took no notice openly, but timed his behaviorisms. Barks occurred at the rate of two to five a minute, and gestures much more frequently. They seemed to reduce tension and occurred more often, I thought, when tests became too difficult. He threw his arms out spastically, throwing his pencil four feet in the air. This action seemed to be involuntary, and he drew his arms back down to his sides in time to catch the pencil on the fly. All this motion occurred while working on the test on which he was doing well.

He knew a lot of boxing lore and talked of paleontology. He's bright, I thought, and has a lot more on the ball than he reveals on tests. At one point, I asked him about his sounds. He stuck his thumb inside his teeth and spit out a string of glottal filth, and I knew who it was intended for. "Slap me," he screamed.

His fantasies were themes of violence and criminal offenses. Yet, his heros always paid the price to father, society, or God. Punishment was always harsh in the fantasies, and sometimes sons retaliated and killed their fathers. One picture used in testing showed an older man seated beside a younger one. Jeff struck the card repeatedly and with such force that I knew he'd hurt his hand. And, in response to a picture of a boy seated forlornly on some steps, Jeff told a story of a boy abandoned by his parents. The child in his story searched for miles and then sat down and wept: "They'll never, never, never come back."

For the purpose of further observing Jeff, I stood, concealed, outside the classroom door and watched the lesson going on. Jeff was in good form that day. A stopwatch in my hand, I counted ten barks in as many minutes. And then he saw me standing there and knew exactly why I'd come, so he put on a show. Four times each minute his shouts rang out, and fingers and arms kept busy, too. I noted all this down, objectively. Whatever else was plaguing Jeff, I saw that he had control and used his symptom selectively. The other children laughed out loud, delighted with the disruption. Jeff was a clown who could reliably break up the tedium of any class. Mrs. Williams had had enough and threw him out once more. He twirled and gestured as he left, proud that he had won.

He strutted right to the principal's door. He flouted

his triumph in her face and received his mock punishment. Whatever mess his life had been, whatever twisted threads of hate propelled him to provoke, whatever unseen nervous impulse sprang from some defective cell within his brain, I knew that Jeff had learned to use this tic to find the attention that he craved.

I built a simple box that lit up whenever I threw a switch. I tore the hour and minute hands from an old discarded clock but left the second hand intact. Every day Jeff and I sat down face-to-face and talked. For each time the second hand went around and Jeff had neither barked nor cursed nor gestured in some new offensive way; and if he kept his tongue within his mouth, his hands folded calmly in his lap; and if he did not act like some demented fool; I switched the light on, and recorded each success. Later, we counted these successes, and he was paid with lemon drops. In no time at all, he showed me I was right; he could control the outbursts for ten or twenty minutes at a time.

The psychiatrist was not impressed. "Repressing it all," he concluded. "He'll just let it come out later." And he did, but only when he had an audience who laughed and cheered and got upset. A young and innocent student-teacher type was best, because she got embarrassed and turned red. But, when I had him calmed, there were no tics or symptoms substituted, or straining effort to control, or sudden burst of epithets when we were through.

The next step was to make it work within the classroom. I had to change the reactions Jeff elicited in the other kids. Instead of laughing when he barked, I wanted them to give support when he behaved appropriately. I hung my box high up on the blackboard, with the clock close by, so all could see.

"I need your help for someone here," I said, "someone who's learned to be a clown and doesn't use his brain the way he should. It's Jeff who needs the help, and without you, he'll not improve."

Again, I counted up the lights recording Jeff's successes, and gave out my rewards. But now the whole class shared in every minute Jeff sat quietly. They took the bait and, reacting as I'd planned, began to cheer him on, delighted as they saw some change. Each day I returned to play the little game. It was not perfect, but it worked. Jeff learned that there were other ways to be noticed and be recognized. His teacher and his classmates found that Jeff could use some self-control.

I gradually weaned myself away.

"You'll never know when I am here," I warned. "I'll listen in on your class, and if there are no barks, I'll come with prizes for all of you."

For weeks I came by every day at hours chosen randomly and listened through an intercom; then, bursting in upon them, I played a Santa Claus role. Jeff got some special things like auto magazines, boxing gloves, and rocks to classify.

We trained his teacher to say, "That's good," instead of engaging in yelling and hysteria. She was to ignore dirty talk since words are not like sticks and stones.

He really did do better in school. But in his dormitory, things did not work out as well, while he was being treated "therapeutically." When he would run away from school because it was too hard, or life seemed easier outside, they'd keep him in the dorm to "gain control." "He was too disturbed for school that day," they would say.

Jeff stayed another year or so, and things remained about the same until his family found another school. I wrote an article with graphs and charts and things that teachers ought to do with Tourette syndrome children.

My telephone rang once late at night. "I hear you know about the condition I have, and I'd like you to treat me."

"What is your condition?"

"Tourette Syndrome—(bark)—I've had it all my life."

"But do you work or go to school?"

"I live at home—(bark)—with my parents. The government pays me every month because of my condition. I was in the service, you see."

"And if you were to improve so that you never said those words again, or barked, or gestured with your hands . . .?"

"I'd lose my pension, then, of course."

"It seems to me that they are paying you to bark. I knew a boy once who got paid off, too."

"I thought you'd like to treat me for scientific reasons. You'd learn a lot about what makes me tick."

"I'm sorry, I can't help you," I returned.

12
Under the Fig Tree

"And they shall sit every man under his vine and under his fig-tree; and none shall make them afraid." ISAIAH II.

She sat rigidly in the padded leather chair across from me, and I could feel her tension. An intense, troubled seventh grader, Abbie was suffering with severe migraine-like headaches three to four times each week. She had undergone a complete physical and neurological examination, but the findings were negative. Her doctor suggested that the headaches were of psychological origin and sent her to see me.

The evidence for a psychogenic basis for the symptom seemed convincing. Abbie was the older of two children. Her parents were both college educated, and the family valued intellectual and academic achievement. The headaches occurred on school days, never on weekends or holidays. School performance was an emotionally-charged area. Abbie had hidden poor grades from her parents and, when discovered, broke down into hysterical crying spells. Her younger brother, Sam, was nine. He was a good student but hyperactive in school. Like many younger brothers, he was a thorn in Abbie's side. He got into her room and touched her things. He knew exactly what to say to torment and upset her. She "hated" him, she said.

I had already completed a psychological evaluation. Abbie was bright enough. She had a rich vocabulary. Her memory was above average, and she showed good conceptual ability. In addition, she was an imaginative child with creative ability. Why, then, were her grades only mediocre?

I found my answer in the projective tests of personality. Abbie seemed conflicted and anxious, despite a happy and bubbly exterior. Test results suggested a rigidly perfectionistic, tightly controlled personality. The projective stories she told suggested a sense of insecurity about her status in the family. Anger and resentment were expressed toward her brother. Abbie was the older child, and apparently never really adjusted to the loss of her privileged position when Sammy was born. One way she could gain parental approval was by academic success. She harbored lofty ambitions to save the world. She would become a missionary and teacher, traveling among primitive tribes and backward peoples, spreading culture and understanding. At other times, she daydreamed of being a poor but talented artist who would one day be discovered.

However, fantasy and reality are often far apart. The more Abbie dreamed, the less success she had in school. Her lofty aspirations also aroused painful fears of failure. She sensed that she was really imperfect, that she could never meet her self-imposed standards. Poor school grades left her feeling humiliated. She exaggerated her defeats and minimized her successes. She began to feel inadequate and dependent upon her parents' affection and support.

Her insecurity emerged in recurrent nightmares

and fantasies of robbers and monsters lurking in the dark. Her relationships with her parents reflected both aspects of her conflict. If she awoke at night, crying because of a throbbing headache, her father came and comforted her until she fell asleep again. Yet, she seemed to harbor feelings of resentment for the pressures her parents placed on her.

When shown a picture of a mother simply reading to her little girl, Abbie told a different tale. In Abbie's story, a mother sends her child to school despite the fact that she is weak and sickly. The child catches cold and dies. The mother never forgives herself.

For Abbie, pressures mounted until her body, in its wisdom, found a way to express quite vividly the tension that she felt. Her anger and fear exploded regularly where Abbie felt most insecure—the seat of intellect and striving and all she held important—her head. How could I be so sure? To every inkblot in my test, Abbie included one telltale response. On every card within the colored, inky spots, she found a monstrous beetle sitting with enormous pinchers sticking out directly from its head.

"Just sit back in the chair, Abbie, and try to relax."

I went through the muscle relaxation procedure that had been described by Jacobsen and later by Wolpe.

"When you are tense, your muscles are tense. If you want to learn how to relax, you must first learn to relax your muscles. It's really very simple. I want you to see how it feels. Sit back in that reclining chair and make yourself comfortable. Fine. Now I want you to clench both of your fists. Good, now hold it. O.K., relax. Do you feel the difference? Now, tense the muscles of your forearm. Hold it, and let go. Notice the difference in the way your muscles feel when you are tense compared with when you relax."

One by one, I proceeded through different muscle groups until Abbie had alternately tensed and relaxed all of the major muscle systems in her body. The next step was to teach her to relax each part of her body voluntarily. I would have Abbie practice this procedure until it became automatic, and she could use it herself as a tension-reducing procedure.

"Abbie, I want you to relax your fingers. Imagine that all of the muscles in your fingers have gone limp. Just let your fingers hang loose. Imagine your hands are just hanging free. Your hand is like a water spigot. All of the tension is spilling out of your finger tips. Just let your fingers relax. That's fine. Now let that nice relaxed feeling in your fingers spread slowly up your hand to your wrist."

Soothingly, and in this manner, I talked Abbie through each part of her body, coaxing her to let herself go, to allow herself to relax. Gradually, I saw her face change as a more peaceful countenance replaced the strained mask she had presented at first. I paid special attention to the muscles of her head and scalp, since this was where her tension was focused when she was most upset.

Several sessions were devoted to relaxation procedures. Abbie was also asked to practice the exercise at home. Finally, I felt Abbie had learned the technique, and I was ready to begin the desensitization procedure.

Systematic desensitization is a technique for dealing with specific fears or tension, and was first developed by a behavioral psychiatrist named Joseph Wolpe. The method is part of a general approach to psychotherapy based upon principles of learning. One way of eliminating an undesirable behavior is to teach the individual a response incompatible with that behavior.

In overcoming phobias, it is advantageous to teach the individual a relaxation response to the situation that normally arouses fear. One cannot be relaxed and fearful at the same time. It is assumed that all fears are learned and can be "extinguished" under the appropriate conditions.

Systematic desensitization involves a direct attack upon the fearful response. It consists of two steps: first, teaching a general muscle relaxation; second, gradual introduction of the fearful stimulus, usually in imagination, while the individual is in a relaxed state. The effectiveness of the technique has been studied experimentally more than any other therapeutic procedure, and has proven to be a very powerful strategy for deconditioning phobias.

"Abbie, you are now perfectly relaxed. See if you can maintain this feeling while we proceed with the next step. Keep your eyes closed and try to follow my directions. I am going to describe a scene for you. Your job is to try to visualize this scene just as if it were real. Imagine yourself doing just what I say, or seeing just what I describe. Try to maintain your relaxation while you imagine the scene. However, if you feel yourself getting tense, even a little bit tense, let me know immediately by raising the index finger on your right hand. As soon as you signal me, I will tell you to stop thinking of that scene and to relax yourself. Do you understand? Good. If you do not signal me, I will assume that you are still relaxed and will go on describing other scenes. Are you ready to begin? Fine.

"I want you to imagine you are sitting in Science class. Think of it just the way it really is at school. Your teacher is lecturing to you at the blackboard. He is unrolling a chart that shows the circulatory system. Just think of yourself listening to the teacher and watching what he is doing. Look at the chart. See the heart and blood vessels. That's fine. You are not signaling me, so I assume you are still relaxed. Let's wipe that scene out now and go on to the next.

"You are still in Science class, but the teacher has asked a question of the class. No one raises his hand. You don't know the answer either. He is looking around the room trying to decide who to call on. He is looking in your direction."

The second phase of systematic desensitization consists of a procedure designed to decondition the individual to the specific situations which normally elicit fear or tension. Because people tend to avoid things that frighten them, they often deny themselves the opportunity to extinguish fear or anxiety. Someone with an airplane phobia usually travels by train or bus. Sometimes the individual cannot avoid a frightening situation, and, in each case, the fear is aroused but at a level so high that the fear does not extinguish. It is advantageous to expose fearful people to the stimuli that frighten them in small and gradual doses. Fantasy or imagination provides a means of accomplishing this without unduly frightening the individual.

Beginning with a relatively neutral scene, the therapist slowly introduces more and more frightening situations. Each step in the procedure is introduced only after the client has been able to imagine previous situations without experiencing tension.

The arousal of a fantasized situation during a period of relaxation may serve to extinguish the anxiety typically aroused by a real situation. Since experience in any real situation also involves thinking about it, fantasy and reality share many common elements. In most phobic individuals, merely thinking about something is sufficient to evoke tense feelings. With practice, however, the client is gradually able to imagine the situation with diminishing amounts of anxiety, and, finally, to imagine it with no anxiety at all. At this point the therapist proceeds to a slightly more frightening situation. For each fear reported by the client, a hierarchy of situations is constructed, varying in intensity along a dimension of time, distance, or other pertinent variable.

As the client completes one level along the dimension, the therapist proceeds to the next level. Eventually, the client is able to imagine the most fearful situation in the hierarchy without experiencing fear. In most cases the training generalizes from the imaginary to the real situation. The client finds that he can now expose himself to the original stimulus situation without being frightened or tense.

I asked Abbie to keep a record on her calendar noting each day she had a headache and each day she did not. We would evaluate the effectiveness of the treatment by the percentage of "headache days" each week and each month. We also worked out a numerical system from zero to one hundred by which Abbie could tell me quickly how tense she felt at any given moment or in any specific situation.

During the next few sessions, Abbie and I worked out a series of "fear hierarchies," which represented the most frightening or tension producing situations she encountered each day. We were able to group these into five broad categories, which seemed to account for most of her daily tension. I labeled them for the sake of convenience: crowds; school; medical; darkness; and anger-frustration.

Abbie's fear of crowds apparently went back many years to numerous experiences in which she was pushed and shoved in crowded buses, theaters, or stores. She had persistent fears of being knocked down and walked over. After many questions and much discussion, we were able to arrange seven specific crowd situations into a dimension ranging from least to most frightening. At the top of the list, and the least frightening for Abbie, was sitting in a crowded movie theater. Even this, however, aroused a mild apprehension. The most frightening situation was the prospect of jamming her way into the school entrance, especially if she were carrying books.

The school fears included such situations as being called upon in class, taking examinations, receiving poor grades, and hearing her teacher yell.

Abbie's medical and doctor fears concerned injections, medical charts and illustrations, fears of accidents and injury, and concerns that her headaches were associated with some horrible medical condition.

Abbie was afraid of the dark, and was especially fearful of being left at home alone at night. Her fantasies about darkness included being chased by a vicious dog who lived up the street and sometimes escaped from his leash.

Finally, there was a group of situations in which Abbie was more angry than scared, but her angry feelings aroused tension because of their association with unpleasant consequences. They included feelings of irritation and resentment toward her brother, especially when he touched her things. Abbie was tense whenever they fought, and especially when her parents responded by accusing and hollering at Abbie.

Subsequent sessions were devoted to practicing relaxation responses and desensitization to the situations described in the five fear hierarchies. When Abbie achieved a relaxed state, I asked her to imagine the lowest item in the series. She was told to immerse herself in the situation as if it were really happening. As she fantasized, she was to signal if she should start to feel tension. On those occasions, I asked her to stop thinking about the situation, and, instead, to think of something calm and relaxing. When Abbie was again calm, I reintroduced the original scene. In most instances, after several practice trials, Abbie could think of a previously frightening situation without experiencing tension.

Prior to beginning therapy, Abbie had been experiencing three to four severe headaches each week. This symptom dated back to her earliest school experiences. Often she awoke during the night with a severe headache. Her extreme fear reaction to a headache was sufficient to concern the parents, and usually to keep them up with her during these times. Her father sometimes rubbed her back to soothe and quiet her.

Abbie's sessions were scheduled twice each week. By the sixth therapy session, we began seeing some changes. She had gone an entire week, headache free. Her parents indicated that this was the longest stretch she had ever gone during a school year without headaches. I knew we were on the right track. Many of the items that Abbie had specified in her hierarchies represented situations that occurred frequently in her life. Her squeamishness about blood and things anatomical was associated with frequent dissections of frogs and other animals, which her brother and father engaged in as a hobby. Abbie participated in these activities with her father, but had never revealed to him how uncomfortable she felt about what she was doing. In addition, the hygiene teacher at school had been discussing anatomy with the use of medical illustrations.

That the therapy sessions were having an effect upon the headaches became vividly clear. Encouraged by the initial improvement, I attempted to speed up the process. Since medical illustrations were frightening, I believed I could achieve a more rapid desensitization by using real pictures rather than Abbie's imagined representatives of such material. The use of the real stimulus, rather than a fantasized situation, is a more rapid form of desensitization, but the danger of going too fast is increased and, rather than reducing fear, may increase it. It is for this very reason that the fantasy procedure is more commonly attempted.

When Abbie had achieved a deep level of relaxation, I asked her to open her eyes. Maintaining her in a relaxed state as much as possible, I presented her with a book of bird pictures to thumb through. She was able to do this, and at the same time, remain relaxed. I then substituted for the bird book Grey's *Anatomy*, the standard anatomical text of medical students. Abbie was told to thumb through the book, page by page. She was to examine each illustration carefully, being sure to maintain her state of relaxation. At the first hint of tension, she was to close the book, close her eyes, and think of something calming. Abbie went through several embryological pictures with interest, denying any tension. When she came to a cut-away of the human abdomen in full color, she signaled tension. I asked her to close the book and spent several minutes relaxing her once more. Again we tried the book. This time she examined several anatomical pictures and reported no tension.

This procedure was continued during the seventh and eighth therapy sessions. Abbie reported that she had gotten tense in school when the hygiene teacher was discussing birth defects, and especially when he displayed a picture of a deformed Siamese twin embryo, which Abbie described as "awful looking." I knew that this was a loaded area in the family because of her uncle who was mentally retarded. How much Abbie had tuned in to these family concerns, I did not know. In any event, she indicated that she had practiced the relaxing exercises during the frightening hygiene class, and they had worked.

Then the headaches began again with all their old fury. At the eighth session Abbie reported she had suffered two bad headaches the preceding week. The first was on a day she was to receive a test grade. It had been a surprise test, and Abbie believed she had failed. As it turned out, she received the second highest grade in the class. The headache came about 5:30 in the evening. Abbie was able to sleep for an hour, but, when she awoke, she still had the pain. The second headache was a milder one, which she experienced for about two hours at school the following day.

Between the eighth and ninth sessions, Abbie again had two headaches. The first occurred on the day she received her report card. She had been tense all day. She related the second headache to concern about a girlfriend, whose parents were divorced, and who was having numerous problems.

I became concerned that the headaches were increasing. There were several possibilities: some sessions she had missed because of a snow storm, the recent focus on embryos, the pregnancy of Abbie's aunt, my use of anatomical pictures rather than fantasizing. I believed the anatomy text to be more frightening than I had imagined. I decided to discontinue the use of the textbook and to return to the original fantasy procedure. I also met with Abbie's parents and asked them to de-emphasize the discussions of medical and biological topics at home, and to perform the frog dissections only when Abbie was away.

Between the ninth and tenth session Abbie had

another headache. It seemed to be related to two events which made her "nervous." That evening she had a bas mitzvah party to attend. She would have to get dressed up, and any clothes other than jeans were objectionable to her. During school that day, the hygiene teacher was discussing hemophilia as an incurable disease, which is also sex-linked. Abbie had done a report with her father's help the evening before using *Scientific American* as her source. In addition to her general fears of medical topics and incurable birth defects, Abbie was also concerned about the onset of menstruation which she felt was overdue. She informed me that if a girl had hemophilia, she would probably die with her first period.

In addition to the fear hierarchy, I found it advisable to have Abbie imagine scenes in which she "told off" teachers who were being mean to her. Although she knew it would be unwise to actually tell off a teacher, the imaginary situation gave some sanction and practice in assertive behavior. It made the teacher less fearsome to her.

At the next session Abbie reported a five-day span with no headaches, the longest since I had introduced the anatomy book. Three events had transpired which I felt would ordinarily have been sufficient to produce tension and headaches. Abbie's girlfriend came to her crying with the information that the girlfriend's grandmother had died. Abbie consoled her. In addition, there was an accident near her school. A thirteen-year-old boy was killed by a bus. The rumors were flying that he had a retarded brother. Finally, Abbie had gotten a small metal splinter in her foot which her father removed with a sharp tweezers. Abbie was tense during this procedure, but was able to control her anxiety by relaxing between probes with the tweezers. We continued to practice the expression of anger by fantasy and role playing. We discussed the importance of expressing feelings rather than bottling them up. Abbie's parents reported that she was becoming more open in communicating with them at home.

No one develops problems by one's self. Often the individual is merely the visible target, expressing problems that characterize the entire family. Abbie's mother had a history of migraine-like headaches, particularly after a tense day at work. Her father's interest in medicine and biology may have been related to his own underlying medical concerns. His own father had died of a heart attack on his fortieth birthday. Abbie's father was now thirty-nine, and may have been experiencing tension about the possibility of his own death.

By the fourteenth session Abbie had gone fourteen days without a headache. We were role playing aggressive and angry roles regularly. These included simulated situations such as being awakened repeatedly by someone dialing a wrong number, and being short-changed in a restaurant. Abbie listened to tapes of other people playing the same roles, and could detect differences among people in their ability to express anger. We also played the situation in which her brother initiated medical discussions at the dinner table. Abbie was rehearsed in asking him politely to change the subject. Finally, we practiced arithmetic tests. I became the teacher and harassed Abbie during the "test." She practiced relaxing and taking her time, while tuning out the interfering distractions.

Abbie's grades seemed to be improving. She began receiving A's on math tests, and earned the highest score she had ever received on a city-wide achievement test. She seemed comfortable, relaxed and happy. She was keeping her own graphs on headache-free days, and she enjoyed listening to herself express anger on the tape recordings we made together. There was little doubt that she was improving in the vehemence with which she could express anger. I mentioned the likelihood of reducing the frequency of therapy sessions in the near future.

At the fifteenth session Abbie had another headache. It began just before our session. While driving to my office, Abbie's mother informed her that she would have a new cousin the next day. Her aunt was scheduled for a Caesarian delivery. Her mother later told me they were very tense about this delivery because of the possibility of mental retardation.

I relaxed Abbie and asked her to focus upon the part of her head that hurt. She was to imagine a circle of pain and, while relaxing, to imagine that circle growing progressively smaller. We did this until I asked her to imagine that the pain was only a small point. I then suggested that it would disappear completely. Abbie reported that her headache was gone but expressed the concern that it might return. I told her that the headache was likely to be related to her concerns about her new cousin. I explained that she could use the same method to deal with headaches whenever they occurred. The demonstration that she had some power over her symptom was extremely important since she usually felt helpless in the face of a headache. I emphasized her role, rather than mine, in eliminating the headache. In subsequent sessions, we practiced this technique. Abbie imagined she had a headache, and then practiced eliminating it.

At the sixteenth session I made a contract with Abbie. If she could go fifteen days symptom-free, we would cut down to once-a-week sessions. During the next few sessions, I began to deal more directly with Abbie's fears of the dark by using actual excursions into darkness from my office. Within a few weeks, she was able to walk several blocks from my office down a darkened street without fear.

Why is a symptom learned by one individual, and another symptom by someone else? Usually, we can only speculate. Some theorists have suggested an "organ weakness" hypothesis to account for individual differences. Abbie remembered two early memories of being injured. In the first, she was taking a bath with her brother when her mother spilled boiling water on her legs. She was only two years old, but recalls staying with her grandmother while her mother rushed to the hospital to get bandages.

About a year later, Abbie cut her head on the leg of a chair. She was dripping blood and was taken to the hospital where she received seven stitches. She remembers screaming: "I want Mommy," and being told by a nurse, "You can't cry; you're a big girl now." While the stitching was going on, Abbie was told that they were putting bitter herbs on her head. She also remembers a large bandage. It is tempting to speculate that Abbie learned at this time to associate head pain and pressure with psychological tension. She had many occasions to relive this fear by identifying with her brother who seemed accident prone and suffered numerous injuries.

Abbie continued to receive good grades and to make progress in handling darkness situations. I began a procedure in which each family member rated every other member each day, according to how tense they appeared. Abbie was receiving consistently low ratings from her family. By the twentieth therapy session, she had gone sixteen days without headaches, and we decreased the frequency of therapy according to our agreement.

Abbie went thirty-six days before her next headache, which occurred after she learned that her dog was pregnant. She next had a twenty-eight day span, and this headache occurred when her dog had pups.

During the next few months, I saw Abbie about once a month. She was still having about one headache a month. She seemed less tense. Her grades had improved from B's and C's to A's and B's. She seemed less compulsive about her schoolwork. In contrast to the original incidents before starting treatment, in which she had hidden her poor grades from her parents, Abbie now seemed less concerned about grades. She was more open in expressing feelings and less upset by her brother. Her last therapy session occurred six months after starting treatment.

Abbie worked for me last summer, teaching retarded children to talk. She's graduated college now. Her headaches have not returned.

13

He Can't Say No

The tall, disheveled student was awkward and uneasy as he entered the room. He clutched the wrinkled appointment slip in his hand. He had arrived, as scheduled, for his interview with the psychologist, a rather common occurrence within an institution for the mentally retarded. We watched the proceedings carefully from behind the one-way screen.

"We'd like to have you do some things for us today," Lucky explained.

She'd gone through this act some twenty times before and would repeat it many more times until we had our sample. We were finally putting to a test the measures so carefully worked out—new ways to study people who'd lived within the sheltered school for most their lives. New ways to label and assess the things that failure and rejection and protection and institutions do.

"I have a contract here that you won't understand. It's all legal and authentic. See, there's an official seal. I'd like you to sign your name right here. Just take my word for it. There, that's fine. You certainly write well."

Lucky walked over to the table on which lay a large black box. She turned a switch, then juggled a knob or two, and it began to hum. Not a soft, peaceful sound like from some old familiar clock or a TV warming up, but a raucous, blasting "hummm" like a dentist's high speed drill. A single coil of wire hung conspicuously from the back with some gleaming copper strands exposed at the farthest end.

"That's 220 volts of electricity," she stated casually. "Please touch it and hold on, until I say let go."

Dutifully, the student rose and grasped the metal strands between two finger tips. The wire, of course, was dead, but this remained unsaid.

"That's fine. You can let go now. Did you feel the shock?"

"It hurt," he answered, mechanically.

"Well, forget it now. It's over. But I have something here that will make you feel all right. Just take this pill. You see, it's pink. I've got a bottle full of them. They're from the pharmacy."

Without hesitating, he took the tiny pill which might have been Stellazine, Tofranil, Valium, "coc," or God-knows-what-else, but was only sugar.

"I want you to make X's in all these little boxes. There are only about 10,000 or so. Just keep on marking them. I'm going out to lunch. I guess you'll have to stay here all alone. Oh, gee, I wonder where that noise is coming from. I hope it won't disturb you. Just keep on working till you're done, then you can leave."

We watched him work, unseen behind the glass, and timed how long he stayed and counted what he marked.

There were other tests as well. Questions that we asked about the things he liked and didn't like. We totaled up the times he answered, "Yes." In other ways we tried to learn if subjects saw themselves as assertive or submissive by asking "If you were on a team, would you be the captain?"

It is generally assumed that the mentally retarded are gullible, compliant, and submissive. If this is so, then opening up the institution door would leave them prey to exploitation and abuse. We worried about this, too.

We also worried about their helplessness, their low degrees of self-esteem, behaviors that were inappropriate and labeled as bizarre, and deficits in learning in areas of sexual roles and functionings.

It all started in 1964, when we applied for and received a sum of money to study the effectiveness of rehabilitation programs for the mentally retarded living within the institutional setting.

For years the institution had been a tight custodial place where children came because parents, schools, courts, and social agencies decided they could not learn or were otherwise unfit. They were labeled "defective," and put in a segregated place way out in the country. Within the sheltering walls, they grew vegetables on farms, repaired shoes, and manufactured brooms and mattresses. Some shoveled coal into antiquated furnaces, cut the grass, did the laundry at big tubs, or worked in kitchens.

Some had parents who came on Visitors' Day, looking embarrassed. Some stood by the roads and watched the cars, expecting parents who never came. Some no longer had any parents, but wrote letters to some memory of a social worker who had placed them there for "training."

Sometimes the parents would decide to take them home and get them jobs so they could be part of a family. A few would run away; and, if they ran far enough, and weren't seen by State Police "thumbing it" down some road leading to anywhere, they made it on their own. But most remained within the institution which became their home, and, though the staff changed from year to year, and buildings were erected or torn down, they went on forever, growing older but not smarter.

During World War II, we needed men. A number of boys volunteered, and draft boards weren't too particular if they came from places with high walls and toilets that had no doors. The barracks weren't much different, and the retarded soldier already knew about listening to orders and marching in straight lines. These boys grew up in uniform and did their jobs well; the institution hung a flag of blue stars, and the school principal wrote an article about the mentally retarded boys who served. And others worked in factories and made machines of war and found it wasn't so different from work they already knew.

Later there were parents' groups that lobbied, and laws were passed. Money found its way to places that heretofore had barely subsisted economically. "Rehabilitation" became the new watchword. There was vocational training in jobs that the retarded were suited for. "Teach 'em about the world of work and how to adjust outside." Workshops, trade training, counseling, remedial education, rehabilitation. Forget the medical terms like "idiot" and "imbecile." It's what they can do that counts. It's their *behavior* that's retarded, and we can change all that. Rehabilitation.

We started our study with a follow-up of people leaving the institution. We went to see them in their boarding houses and apartments, or sometimes at the "Y." We asked a lot of questions about their jobs, the friends they'd made, and how they spent their time. We asked to see their paychecks, the rental slips, bank books, and withholding forms. If they let us, we would snoop around a little and see their furniture and look at what they'd hung up on their walls.

We asked them about their jobs, the people with whom they worked, and whether they rode the bus or took a trolley home. And, we asked if they paid their rent on time, or voted, or borrowed money, or drove a car, or used a bank.

We punched it all on cards and fed it to the Univac and wrote down the results in tables that filled a fat, impressive-looking book.

The retarded and illiterate who had spent their lives behind the walls did not disintegrate when let out in the world. They became janitors, or factory hands or kitchen help, and blended into the melting pot like everybody else. They married, reproduced, and paid their bills. They stayed employed, cashed their checks, and sometimes changed their jobs or got promoted. They maintained themselves outside of institutions and did not break the law. Sometimes they lost their jobs, had children illegitimately, smashed their cars, or gave their money for insurance or encyclopedias they really didn't need. They weren't always satisfied with the salary they earned or the scutwork positions they were given, or never getting ahead. But, mostly they survived.

Before they left, we tried to find a way to identify the ones who would fare the best, and those who would need financial aid, or someone to bail them out. So we gave them hours of IQ tests and measured what they had learned in school, and determined how fast they could put round pegs in holes. We asked the people who instructed them to push a broom or run a press to tell us who they thought would make it, and who would not. Then, we correlated scores and ratings and whatever else we thought might matter with criteria like job stability and wages. At first we thought we found some clues that we might later use to select the people who could leave. But then we did it all again and found it was just artifact. Reluctantly, we conceded that after years of trying, we couldn't predict a thing. No matter whether IQ tests said 55 or 83, no matter whether they could read a "Dick and Jane," or could not read at all, no matter what our raters said, we simply could not tell who would do well in the outside world and who would not.

So we put our heads together and thought about two hundred people that we knew who had once been students at the institution. Some ideas were generated about the ones that could not help themselves when the landlord said, "move out," or a sponger wanted to "move in," or a salesman said, "sign here," or a boyfriend said, "lay down," or they thought about themselves as dumb, or when they acted that way.

We put it all together and wrote a paper that a journal printed about how institutions shelter and protect and maintain behavior which handicaps the handicapped. Then we devised some tests of behavior for acquiescence and helplessness and self-esteem, and used the tests to evaluate those who were still enrolled, but soon would leave.

Then we thought about the teaching and the counseling. We called together groups of students who were often sheeplike and withdrawn and yelled at them in counseling groups for acting weird, or for signing things they did not understand. We put it all down in training manuals to tell others how to counsel and advise, and gave the program a catchy letter name.

Describing it at meetings and in journal articles, we called it "research utilization", and cautioned that those who study people within the institution must make their studies relevant and leave the basic research and the elegant theories to the learned men at universities.

We spoke a lot at meetings and told the staff to put aside their testing kits and make the institution a little more like the community. Sometimes they listened and started counseling groups themselves, and we watched them from one-way windows and said, "That's good!"

14

Lenny's Gone

Lenny never made it out of the institution. One morning, while walking to work along the Pike (he was saving himself the taxi fare), Lenny was hit by a speeding auto. The motorist kept on driving. By the time the ambulance arrived, and the quivering mass of reflexes was finally brought to the emergency room, there was little hope. He died a half hour later.

"I'd like to see a psychologist," he had requested. "I've got a problem. Want to talk to someone about it."

That was the first time a student had ever asked for counseling, at least as long as I could recall. And I'd been there a long time. Oh, we counsel them all right, because their supervisor thinks they need to talk, or when they will not go to school, or if they've hit someone, or have broken a window or two. But students seldom ask to talk just because they know that things are all mixed up inside and need someone to listen.

"Come on in," I invited. "Sit down and let me hear what's on your mind."

It really wasn't hard to help at all. He'd been

assigned to unload trucks, but printing was what he really wanted. I made a call and asked that he be changed. He never forgot the incident, and sometimes returned to talk. Not regularly, he didn't think he needed that. But every now and then he'd show up at my door and let me know about his past and what he hoped to be.

"I can't believe I'm really gonna make it," he told me once. "I know that I'll screw up somehow and be here like the rest."

"Don't worry, Len," I reassured. "Everyone knows the progress that you've made. Another year or two and you'll be gone from here and on your own. Why, pretty soon you'll be coming back to visit, to let us know how well you've done."

"Not me," he said. "I'm never coming back again. I've had enough of institutions."

It was a time of change. Old attitudes were crumbling, and the custodians of the institution were gradually becoming more optimistic. The old words we used were dropping out, like "idiot" and "segregation," "menace," and "shelter." We spoke of rehabilitation and finally acknowledged what had been known before— that many of our students had been denied too long. They could be stock clerks, laborers, orderlies, and janitors; just because they couldn't read or write was no reason to withhold the liberty and the rights that others have. The institution walls came down, and those who previously had had no future were taught to live outside and earn their way.

Lenny had been in the wrong place at the wrong time. Institutionalized as a child, he had lived here most of his life. His mother was a hooker. They said she lived with a black man. The courts took Len away from her when he was only eight. He didn't do so well on the tests that measure intellect and classroom work and

how far one will go in school, and that was all they
needed to send him to the "Training School."

His mother never came or wrote, but Lenny kept
on trying to see her. The social worker tried as well, but
Lenny's mom had her own troubles. Christmas times
were very bad because others left to see their folks, and
Lenny stayed behind. We tried to make it festive, and
there were presents wrapped by volunteers and carol-
ing and a tall spruce with lights that flickered on and off
and Santa came around. But after all, it was still an
institution. Lenny seemed to fight more in December,
and once or twice he ran away, but the State Police are
vigilant, and they know an institution kid when they
see one.

Of course, there were those incidents with the
younger boys, who had been used at night by older,
stronger lads who had no other way. So, when he was
more fully grown, it became his turn to be a man. But
he was trying hard to deal with that and knew that it
was wrong. It wasn't so very long ago when terms like
"moral imbecile" were used by learned men and written
into books. But now we know what institutions do,
and I could counsel with our staff and make them
understand.

Once, when we were working with a group of
younger kids to teach them to behave, Len asked if he
might help. The ones who had cut their meat or eaten
with a fork would earn some little prize—a piece of
gum, some trading cards, a package of balloons, or
other ten-cent Woolworth junk—to make them know
we cared. Len worked beside us pouring milk and giving
praise and, though he never told me so, he was repay-
ing a favor.

I stood by helplessly while Dr. Baker made the call.
"I have some terrible news for you," he said, as

gently as he could. "Your son Leonard died today. It was an automobile that hit him. I'm sorry to have to tell you this."

"My baby," she cried. "My baby."

15
The Institution Was My Home

The school car is a plush white Oldsmobile station wagon with full power. I was driving it for the first time, and I enjoyed the luxury. But joy riding was not my purpose. Margaret sat in the back seat, her one good hand clenched tightly around the hanging strap. I could feel her tension. Marilyn, the rehabilitation counselor sat with me up front. She was the therapist; I had suggested this approach.

I watched Margaret through the rear view mirror and told her to relax. "We'll do nothing that will frighten you," I reassured. "Just let us know when you are scared, and we'll stop whatever we are doing until you feel relaxed again and tell us to begin."

For sixteen of her thirty-seven years the institution had been her home. Her family had broken up. An agency then intervened, and there had been a foster home and then another. But an eleven-year old with cerebral palsy and mental retardation is not an easy kid to place. Her left arm just hung down limply;

135

she felt no sensation there. She also limped. She came
to live at Laurel Hall.

She arrived when things were changing. Rehabilitation became the order of the day, and workshops and
occupational training replaced the old custodial
philosophy. Margaret learned some housekeeping
skills. She worked in the laundry and in the hospital.
She attended classes in the evenings to learn about the
outside world. Sometimes she was taken on community
excursions to see first hand the things we take for
granted—shopping centers, post offices, banks, sub-
ways, restaurants, bowling alleys, and movie theaters.
There's only so much one can learn in classrooms.

Like many who had come before her, we thought
that Margaret soon would leave. Not "cold turkey", but
gradually, with lots of help. First to a halfway house
where she would live a year or so and work at something she could do, learn about the city, and receive
training and counseling. Then, when she was ready,
she'd leave for good. And, if she could not hold her job
or became upset or got confused, there still were ways
to bring her back for further help; and we would try
again.

But Margaret wasn't buying that. She was afraid of
going out, even gradually. Separations always frightened her; the world outside was dangerous. She pan-
icked when she saw a crowd or rode a trolley car.
Department stores were to be avoided at all costs; the
escalator made her shake. She didn't want to leave her
home and friends. It was safe at Laurel Hall, and
though she knew that there was more to living, she was
afraid to try.

We weren't surprised by what she said. The prospect of leaving shelter and protection is always somewhat scary. Other students at the institution had said

as much. For one who's not so steady on her feet, a
crowd's a place where one can wind up being trampled.
And if a hanging, withered arm is one's burden, self-
consciousness is only natural. If one must limp and use
one hand, an escalator is dangerous, and public trans-
portation has high steps and signs that aren't so easy to
understand. The ordinary ways we weaned the students from our grounds were simply not enough. But,
should we let her waste a life that had the potential for
being free, for coming and going whenever she pleased,
for working competitively? No, not when there are
good ways to overcome what frightens and inhibits us.

With great attention to detail, we tried to pinpoint
every fear. When Margaret rode the trolley car, she
thought that she would "throw a fit." (She hadn't had a
seizure in ten years.) She sensed a "tension" in her
useless hand as if it might rise up mysteriously; she felt
obliged to hold it down. And when seated far from the
door, she felt the need to escape. She knew the car
would never reach her stop. In restaurants and stores,
her heart beat fast. She started sweating. She thought
that she'd pass out.

Traditional counseling was ruled out. Margaret
didn't have the words to talk of feelings very well. We
had to deal directly with her phobias. Since fear is
learned in painful ways, its origin may be forgotten. We
avoid the things that frighten us and so we may never
realize they are no longer dangerous. Our strategy was
clear. We had to find a way to re-expose our girl to all
the things that made her shake. We had to do this
gradually without risking further fright, until, in tiny
doses, she could learn to do what terrified. "Desensi-
tize" is the word we used.

"Breathe deeply and relax your muscles." We
practiced that each day.

"As soon as you begin to feel the slightest bit afraid, start doing this. It will become a habit."

"And tell me on a scale from ·one to ten if you are calm or nervous."

We drove her to the discount store. We weren't after bargains. For a quarter of an hour we sat outside, and Margaret thought about entering. At last she said that she would try. We walked along beside her. It was more than encouragement we offered. We were her security. Three times she started then turned back to practice muscle relaxation. The fourth time we made it in. A few feet past the revolving door and out she went again. We stayed all that afternoon and many more until she could go in and out, pick out something nice, pay for it, ask the lady there for help, and even ride the escalator. (That, alone, took a day.) Then, she learned to do all this while we waited apprehensively outside!

That's the way we worked with her, one fear at a time. Once we spent an hour just touching trolley cars. Next we paid to ride one block, then exited. The driver gave us strange looks. But that was nothing compared to the looks we got when we raced it down the street and got on board again.

Six months later Margaret was taken for a trip to Walnut Hall, the halfway apartment house. She stayed for several hours and had her supper there. Walnut Hall is one floor of a residential hotel within the inner city area, where students being trained to leave the institution may live and work and learn to cope with independence. A counselor and his wife are there to supervise, but the residents have their own apartments and lock their doors, so it's not like the institution. The next time Margaret visited, she cooked spaghetti for herself and Marilyn.

We found a job for her at Mercy Hospital; she was

a housekeeping aide and had to join the union. She took the bus each day to get to work. The bus stop was only two blocks up the street from Walnut Hall. We practiced traveling that route each day until she knew the way alone. Next weekend, she moved down to Walnut Hall. There wasn't very much to move. She made the separation from the school without incident.

We heard about the wedding from her friends. Joe grew up at the institution, too, but he's been out for some time now. He learned that she'd been discharged and looked her up. They live downtown, and both are working steadily. Between the two of them, they should make out all right. We see them now and then on special days back at the school, when there are carnivals and the graduates come to visit.

16
Forgiveness of My Sins

Dear Pastor,

How are you today? I want you to know that I was very happy to go to church with you. I have a problem and I was wondering if you could help me with it.

When I first came to ——— I was ten years old and my counselor took us out on the field to have recreation. Four other boys and I were playing cowboys and Indians in the woods. The other boys left and before I noticed their disappearance a man standing behind a tree called me. He asked me to do a homosexual act. I didn't know any better because I was young so I did. He also threatened me.

Because of the experience I can't seem to control that problem today. I've been to doctors and they couldn't help me. I was wondering if you could help me with it.

I would also like you to please see if you can get me out of ——— for good because I see the need for being around prayerful people if I want any of these problems taken care of. My real mother won't go to court to see if she could get me out. I don't know why.

I don't want just to go to church with you once a year but allways and when I come home to you all on the twenty-fourth of July. I will kneel down on the altar and pray and ask forgiveness of my sins.

> Do you rember the day when I asked
> forgiveness of my sins when I was small and I
> cried and cried but after I lost all my faith in
> God in fact I don't know what God is. I can't
> read very well and so I try to read the Bible but I
> can't.
>   Your friend Philip

Change happens slowly within a residential school. Old-fashioned attitudes die hard, and new ideas rebound off stone walls of resistance. "We've always done it this way—the risk is too great—be patient—it'll never work."

But, things have changed since Philip was admitted. There are new dormitories, and the large open woods are no more. The floors are carpeted these days, and students go to dances. In group counseling classes, males as well as females sit in a circle and discuss their feelings.

It wasn't always that way. There was a time when boys would dance with boys and girls with girls. Privacy was not allowed and even toilets had no doors. Sexes were kept apart as if, by preventing contact, some terrible contagion would be avoided.

In those times it was said that masturbation caused pimples. Evil thoughts were not allowed. God help the staff if a parent found his poor retarded daughter pregnant, the one he sent to be sheltered from a hostile world where innocents and mindless incompetents are preyed upon. Yet, we turned away and made little jokes about the boys who got together late at night in Comfort Hall. That had to be expected in such close living situations. What other outlets did they have?

At a meeting with the building staff not so long ago, we talked about the need to teach about making babies and contraception and becoming a man. From the back a hand was raised, and I acknowledged the questioner.

"I agree with all you say," he began. "But tell me, please, why it is that in our building the boys are taught to urinate like girls, by sitting down?"

We checked and, sure enough, the female supervisors said it really is much neater if it's done that way. We talk a lot about women's lib and unisex and changing attitudes and, even here, such ideas find an ear. But, how are boys to learn that they are masculine unless they learn from men what urinals are for?

Clarence left two years ago and got a job. At the Veterans Hospital he cleaned the floors and scrubbed so well that they gave him a commendation and put his picture in their monthly news. He saved enough to buy a brand new Plymouth, fire engine red, and polished it with Simonize several times a week. He paid too much, but he didn't care because it was a sign that he had made it. Despite the parents who abandoned him when he was only seven, despite the years within the Institute (to him that word meant institution), despite the books he could not read, the sums he could not do, despite all the humiliations, he now was free and on his own, and he would show them all. He loved to ride around town showing off his shiny wagon and eyeing the short-skirted girls, the ones he couldn't talk to, but dreamed about.

We watched him once swimming at the hospital pool—a privilege of the staff. When some nurse's aides dove in too, he swam over to the side and pulled himself out.

"What's with you, man? Those girls are cute. I thought you said you're lonely."

"Sure they are, but I don't want to get 'em pregnant."

"You think that swimming in the pool with them is gonna make them pregnant?"

"That's right."

"Now where'd you get a dumb idea like that?"

"Back there at the Institute you never let us swim with girls. I figured that was why."

I was pleasantly surprised when I first encountered Philip. A handsome, dark-haired boy, he hardly looked the part of an institutional resident. But for the technicality that his parents weren't married, he might never have been a student at the school. Rejected by his parents, he grew up in an orphanage. He came to the school when he was seven. New boys sometimes have it tough, and he was no exception. But he learned quickly to adapt.

"I was making out with older boys before I knew what I was doing. Then I found I liked it. When I got bigger, it became my turn to be on top."

"Bed-hopping" is how the students label what goes on at night when staff are not around to supervise. Or if a student wants a quick thrill in the john or out behind a tree, he solicits friends to "take a walk" with him.

But Philip seemed upset about his behavior. He knew that outside people laughed at "queers," and he'd be leaving soon. It wasn't that he wanted to go on that way; he just couldn't find a way to stop. Sometimes the boys came tapping at his door at night. Sometimes he tapped on theirs. Yes, Philip would be leaving soon. He had learned to run a printing press, and soon there would be a job for him outside. He did all right on tests of intellect, and although he didn't really read or write so well, that didn't matter much. Freud said that mental health was being able to love and work. Philip was a very good worker.

He came to his counselor one day and said he needed help. The request went through all the channels and landed in my bin. "Could you counsel Philip to help him with his homosexual problems?"

"I think I can help you," I told him, "but you've got to do as I say. It's not easy to change what you have done for so many years."

I asked him if he masturbated. He didn't understand the word, but when I used a phrase he knew, he said he did it sometimes but knew that it was wrong. I told him it was fine to do until he found a better way to relieve the tension that he felt.

"Just make sure that you do it privately. Not in the open with others watching you, but in the john behind the door, or in your bed at night."

I told him it was normal, that all the boys his age were doing it. It meant that he'd become a man.

He returned next week and said he'd done it seven times, no trouble at all. I praised him for his manly prowess, and he seemed pleased.

"How come I've never seen you at the dances on Wednesday night?"

"I'd like to go, but I'm a little nervous around girls. I never seem to know what I should say."

We spent about a dozen hours dealing with the anxiety that Philip felt. First, in imagination, I described the ways he might encounter girls. He closed his eyes and listened while I talked of seeing them from far away and then up a little closer. He told me when he felt tense, and I would stop. Then he'd relax a bit, and we would start again. He fantasized the ways that he would talk to them and what he'd say. Then, when he

seemed a little calmer, we played the roles out openly. I
was the girl; he was himself. I taught him lines to say.
We used a tape recorder to listen and correct.

A pretty female teacher helped us out. She sat
reading in her office. Philip walked by and looked in
briefly, then turned his head away and kept on walking
by. Ten times we did that until he said he could walk in
and say hello. The teacher smiled and greeted him. He
turned around and left.

Each week he came and practiced until he could go
in and sit and talk with her. At first we had to write out
exactly what he'd say, as well as how she'd answer.
And, if she deviated only slightly from the script, he'd
stutter and walk out. At last he put the script away and
could talk naturally. He said he was afraid no longer.

Together they went to the Campus Shop, and
Philip bought her a Coke. He called the teacher on the
telephone and practiced asking for a date. She taught
him social etiquette and how to do the boogaloo. But,
he knew it was only practice.

We sent him to the weekly dance and went along to
watch. Nervously, he went up to a younger version of
his teacher, a sloe-eyed coquette who looked him up
and down and wasn't shy. They danced the boogaloo.

On street corners and in locker rooms, the
adolescent learns the lore of sex, the things his parents
don't discuss. Much that he learns is far from true; boys
tend to exaggerate, and what is hidden and mysterious
and forbidden and unavailable becomes desirable. Boys
also talk within the institution, and this may be their
only source of information.

Sometimes Philip and I just talked about slang
terms for genitals and intercourse and pregnancy and
contraception. We looked at pink fleshy photographs in
magazines for men and examined a book or two from

stores downtown with male clientele. It wasn't that Philip was disinterested in girls. He just hadn't had much opportunity to find out what he liked.

Psychologists have tried electric shock to make their clients learn to turn away from acts society will not accept. When alternatives are also taught, it has a chance of working.

I made a tape for Philip and had him listen once each week. It described the kinds of things that Philip did with other boys; no words were minced. It also portrayed that which might occur after he left the School, in lavatories or select bars downtown, or in some cruddy rooming house for lonely men. After each enactment of a scene, there were some other things for Philip to imagine. These thoughts were made to nauseate, to frighten, and to curb whatever type of arousal that Philip felt. I hoped to make it painful for him, by some Pavlovian mechanism, so that when ideas of sex with men originated in his thoughts, they'd make him nauseous once again. Inhibited in this approach and still ungratified, he'd have to find another way. Then all the other training that we'd done might help him do things differently.

"Sex education," the faddists cry. "You can't shelter them forever. Teach them to use what God has given them and don't be shy about it. This is a new day, and we need no longer be afraid."

The curriculum was written in great detail, and points were neatly identified by numbers and by letters, so there'd be no mistakes. Large colored anatomical charts were precisely labeled so that every tube and opening had its own Latin name. Sections were devoted to VD, to being careful, ruined reputations, inhibition and control; and every now and then, a moralistic comment was slipped in.

"They need to learn behaviors," I insisted. "Why should they know these names when they can't learn to read or write? Teach them to act and get along with girls. Who cares about the *vas deferens*?"

They called me from the Campus Shop. Philip was there and had created quite a stir. It seems he placed his hands too far around a girl who wore a low cut dress.

"I guess he's over-trained," I said. "We'll have to work on that some more."

"Now look," the Director answered accusingly, "he can't go around here feeling girls. You know the way things are."

"I'm afraid that's your problem now."

17
Dear John Letters

He was not much over four feet tall, and his pristine Munchkin appearance and pleasant disposition made him an institution favorite. He uttered no more than single words and those only in singsong, parrot-like fashion.

At the age of thirty-two John had developed, intellectually, no more than the average three year old. His mental growth had leveled off many years before, and his life within the cloistered setting had not considerably broadened his experience.

Down's Syndrome, sometimes called Mongolism, results from a disorder of the chromosomes. Nature was overly generous here. The twenty-first chromosome, which should be paired, occurs instead in triplicate. The result is mental retardation, moderate-to-severe, and irreversible.

Linda placed the tracing paper over the large block letters and motioned for John to begin. John looked confused. She took his hand and guided the pencil, J... O... H... N; then, placing a fresh sheet of paper over the letters, again gestured toward the pencil. Still no response from John. This time she took the pencil herself and carefully traced each letter, leaving only about a quarter of an inch for John to complete. She eased the pencil back into John's hand and gently nudged him to begin. A glimmer of recognition! Linda knew that, at last, he comprehended. Laboriously, John traced a wiggly pencil stroke, and the "J" was accomplished. He looked up, questioning with his eyes. Linda pointed to the "O." A hesitant sign, a slow passage of hand and pencil through the air, and it was done. This time John did not look up but went directly to the "H" and then the "N." A squeal of delight from Linda; a broad, toothless grin from John.

One of the most fertile areas for the application of behavioral techniques lies in teaching the mentally retarded. Numerous research reports document the successful application of learning principles in teaching traditional classroom subjects, self-help skills, language, or how to improve behavioral adjustment. We wondered whether we could teach a severely retarded man to perform some complex motor acts and visual discriminations using the same strategies.

By means of an elaborate stimulus presentation system, two psychologists were able to teach a severely retarded adult to distinguish between an ellipse and a circle, even when the difference between the two geometric forms was only slight. They developed a teaching program which was so precisely sequenced that learning, almost totally free of error, could occur. We reasoned that discrimination between colors, forms, and letters should be no more difficult than that between circles and ellipses, and would be more useful.

John had been institutionalized at the age of twelve. At the time of admission he could not write his name, identify colors, or give his age correctly. After a short time in the school program, he was judged "uneducable" and excluded from further attempts at education. John was assigned to his dormitory to sort clothing. Twenty years later, his educational level was approximately the same as it had been upon admission.

John lived in a large, open residential setting with a group of men his age, all of whom functioned at about the same intellectual level. Once each day he walked in a line to an Occupational Therapy class where he sanded a piece of wood. Perhaps he did other jobs as well, but every time we visited, John was sanding the same piece of wood.

We asked his houseparents to suggest something that we might teach John, some little task that would improve the way he lived or make him happier. "His parents write him every week," they said. "Was there not some way that we could help him learn to write his weekly letters home? It would so please his parents." Assuming this was far beyond what we could even hope (If John could write, would he have ideas to express?), we reached a compromise. John would learn to print his name. When Mrs. Flynne from Building Four composed the letters home, John could sign them, and Mom and Dad would know that he'd participated, too.

Each day John practiced with "J's" and "O's" and "H's" and "N's". Each day Linda did a little less, and John made up the difference. At first his tracings were a mess; he went from point to point all right, but not, by far, the shortest way. But Linda knew how fast to push, and gradually his hand and eye began to work, and firmer, straighter lines were drawn. At last he traced his whole first name alone; Linda merely told him when. His surname, somewhat longer than the first, he handled with equal dispatch.

Assiduously John came each day for his half an hour alone with Linda, his teacher. In twenty years of

institutional care, it had never been so good. With
tracing underneath his belt, he started copy work. Each
letter was presented as before, a small part at a time.
Within a week the job was done, and John could copy
his name from the model placed before him on the desk.
The next step would prove to be more difficult.

If John were going to learn to print autonomously,
he'd have to give up the big block letters Linda gave him
as a crutch. He'd have to recognize each letter by its
shape and also learn their order.

Eight plastic letters of his name (some appeared
more than one time) were spread out on the table, and
John was taught to pick them out. More were added
after that until he knew them well. And then, he
learned to say their names whenever Linda pointed.
Next Linda made him spell his name J-O-H-N . . .J-O-
H-N, perhaps a thousand times, until associations were
formed and learning was complete. Before the days
when roads were paved, an ancient herder daily led his
flock through tangled underbrush to some distant
waterhole. The constant trampling of their hoofs
forged cow paths through the brush until the vines and
weeds gave up their fight, and the path became a road.
So in John's brain, some paths were laid by dogged
repetition until the minute, nervous discharge aroused
by sight and sound of scrawling lines, which we call
letters, also had their path. Whenever John imaged a "J"
and cell assemblies were aroused in some far cortical
fissure, then "O" soon followed and an "H" and finally
an "N." And virgin pathways along a fibrous tract and
dendrite synapses, hitherto unused, now found a function. Once the "JOHN" became a whole, we started in
again with family name along endless trials until at last
he put it all together. For over thirty years this three-
year old intellect, within the body of a man, sat waiting

for the day when he could place his own identity in letters and tell the world, "It's me. I'm John."

From the day we started work with John, until he wrote his name, more repetitions were required than we cared to count. But, chronologically it took two months and represented more than he had been taught in twenty years. And John retained the skill about as well as a normal man with twenty-three neat pairs of chromosomes.

We built a box to help him learn the differences between the objects of his world. From sets of pictures lined up five at a time, John had to choose the one we asked for. If he chose well, a bell would ring and lights went on as well. On three-by-five-inch index cards we used Magic Markers to draw the colors and forms, letters and words we wanted John to learn.

From randomly numbered tables, we determined which button was to be the correct one, and placed our cards accordingly. A set of problems sequenced logically, from simple to more difficult. This was used as our curriculum. Each step would lead John to the next so that he would not fail, or so we hoped. John was to choose ten times for every problem. If the bell rang nine times he proceeded one step further up the ladder. But, if he failed to hit nine times, he slid back down a step, to repeat what he had previously performed. Then, working his way up again, he'd again try the critical task, and sometimes this was all he'd need to learn from his mistakes. But, if he failed repeatedly, we knew that we had erred. Then we'd go back and think it out and introduce some smaller intervening steps to bridge the gap. We knew we were accountable for what John did learn and what he didn't. Too many errors were demoralizing for all of us. We had to make the program right so others could use it too.

We learned a number of tricks to make it easier for him. The choices had to be so clear they'd shout out, "This way!" "Right here!" We could not otherwise guide him with either language or sign. The first step was to isolate whatever was correct, so John would know which card to press. This card differed from all the rest. We learned to call this an "oddity problem." Whenever we had something to teach to John, like "red" or "square" or "A" or "B," we started it in that way. Then gradually the background changed to a more complicated form. John would have to concentrate just slightly more to keep on being right.

It also was expedient to use whatever John had already learned to teach him something new. For example, if we wanted John to choose a square when we said "square" and it was necessary for him to ignore the circles, stars, and hexagons around it, we'd make the square a red one. John already knew what was red and what was not. "Press the red square, John." Then gradually the other forms acquired a reddish tint, and step-by-step they gradually became redder still. Finally the bright red flag that we had given John was no longer any use to him because all forms were red. But usually John kept right on choosing the square. "Fading" we called this ploy.

The rest was tedious but followed logically. We wrote a step-by-step program which brought John gently along, and if we sequenced steps in increments that weren't too far apart, John would learn.

We started with the simplest task we thought John could do. Without a hitch John picked out "white" from "black" and "black" from "white," and we were on our way.

Colors were next, and progress was fast as we paired every color of the rainbow with every other color, then mixed them all together. Compulsively we charted all the color combinations; nothing was left undone. Initially he did so well that we wondered where all this would end. Until we hit the "red" and "green."

No matter how many times we tried, John could not seem to separate the Christmas colors.

"Why bother?" Linda challenged. "It's obvious he's color blind. They often are you know. Let's go on to more useful things. So he won't master traffic lights, so what?"

The logic of her argument was fine, but I insisted that we try just one more time.

"I think I might just know a way. It won't take long. Bear with me just a bit."

It wasn't stubbornness that nagged me but something I had said before when I addressed a group.

"Don't explain away your failures as mental retardation," I preached. "Why, Skinner teaches rats to play ping pong. And when an animal doesn't learn to run a maze or push a bar, he doesn't say that the organism is defective. He says the program is no good. So don't excuse the fact that children here may not learn to read or print their name by hiding behind some fancy diagnostic label."

What kind of hypocrite would I be, then, to ignore John's color blindness?

We took the bloody stimulus card and withdrew it from the deck. In its place we substituted one that John could find. A small red square was in the center, no bigger than a stamp. Around the red, a fat white border separated red from green. That border was a marker that John could understand. John found this red ten times and never missed and moved on to step two. The red was slightly bigger now, the border shrank a bit. Again John rang the bell ten times.

Repeatedly we played the game, the square

increased in size until at last a fragile white margin remained to mark the way. John never made an error. At last we took away the white and went back to the original red card, the one he couldn't do. With intense concentration, John responded, pondering each choice a good half minute or more. But every time he chose, he chose right. And then to prove our point we did it all again, and John chose "green" from "red."

Color blind or not, John certainly could learn. What implications did this have for further progress? Suppose someone had started teaching John this way when he was ten or eight, or one year old?

Once John knew colors, we taught him squares, rectangles, triangles, circles, ellipses, and other geometric forms. He learned to label them.

John was ready for the alphabet. We divided the letters into equal groups of six or seven each, and worked with four groups separately. Each letter was presented against a background of another, no combination was left out. Each quarter was done separately and then combined in halves, then the halves were intermingled. Eight weeks later John could find any letter out of the twenty-six.

We taught him to discriminate between some simple words like "eye" and "ear" and "nose," and then began a published reading program, which proved to be unwise. Several months went by, and John was midway through a preprimer, but progress had slowed down so much that we became discouraged. We stopped the lessons at that point, except to check up every now and then to see that John could still print his name.

It's been six years since those sessions with John, and other things have taken precedence. John has grown older without a teacher all his own for half an hour a day. I still wonder how far he might have gone had we tried paths other than reading, which we didn't program well.

I saw John yesterday. We brought some visitors through Centennial, where he lives now. The recreation team was there, and John threw a bean bag toward a target on the floor. I said hello, and he smiled back, but I think he was just being polite.

18
Happy Talk

"The wheels on the bus go round and round, round and round, round and round. The wheels on the bus go round and round, all through the day."

The children joined in the singing any way they could. The brightest mouthed the words and made the hand gestures enthusiastically, their eyes fixed on the teacher for clues to the next verse. Those who could not articulate hummed along, keeping time to the music with their bodies. A few children merely sat, while an aide moved their hands to be the wheels and driver and windshield wiper.

This was the pre-school language class—fourteen children, between the ages of three to five, accepted because they did not talk. The classroom was designed to stimulate speech with daily individual language training for each child, and weekly counseling for parents. The formula had proven successful for dozens of children handicapped by whatever it is we label mental retardation, brain damage, emotional disturbance.

We were not overly concerned about diagnosis. It mattered little what pigeon holes we put the children in to ease our insecurity about what we can't understand. Labels don't explain a thing, and we had long since learned that teaching three year olds to talk, when

159

somehow nature was neglectful or merely tardy, does not depend on nomenclature.

Jimmy had entered the program five months ago. A large, attractive four year old, he could not seem to concentrate. While others sat in little plastic chairs around the teacher, Jimmy wandered about the room and found some way to draw attention to himself. Sometimes he pulled off all his clothes and hid them until the teacher, who had better things to do, would search each corner of the room and finally pull a dripping sock out of the toilet bowl. Then Jimmy laughed devilishly; he loved preschool.

He seemed to understand all right but never tried to talk except to say "bye-bye," no matter what he meant. I saw him every day alone, and progress had been slow. I was using a method tried many times before with other children who were mute, or babbled without words, or said a word just now and then, or said a slew of words just once and never twice. For most of these children our method had been good. The method was to make language positive by praise and M&M's and lots of attention. "That's good talking, Joey." Go slowly, one sound at a time, then put them all together in syllables and words and phrases and sentences. Sometimes it took a year or more of tedious repetition with long lists of words until the child learned a vocabulary. Then we would start again with sentences, so that the rules which we call grammar become a part of him. Sometimes a breakthrough happened quickly, because the child already understood and had the apparatus to say the words out loud, but hadn't been motivated.

Perhaps parents were clever enough to interpret grunts and gestures and a child didn't need to talk. Or perhaps parents became so emotional that the child grew intimidated and refused to try. Whatever the cause, with the simple expedient of praise and with other children learning too, going very slowly so that we never demanded more than he could do, a child would become verbal. Sometimes it was like lightning and in a matter of weeks a child who'd been silent began to label everything around him. Then frustrated temper outbursts gave way to more effective language.

It didn't go so well with Jimmy. Stubborn and negative, he found ways to sabotage. I grew angry at his opposition because he was so good at it. Then I was angry at myself for letting a retarded child annoy me so. "He's got to sit and look me in the eye, before he'll learn to talk," I told his father. I counseled with the parents every week and asked them to do, at home, what we were doing here.

"Language must be learned by practice," I explained. "The more trials he has, the faster he will learn, like any other skill. So you must work at home each day with him, and what we do will generalize. And when you find that you have been effective and Jimmy starts to say words you taught him, then you'll feel better too."

It had worked that way before and parents who'd felt helpless and depressed, because their child wouldn't be like other kids, were usually able to learn that they had some power to help.

Psychologists and social workers, who counsel parents of retarded kids, may do some good by expressing sympathy to parents and asking them how bad they feel and how they felt when they found out their child was not like all the rest. But this does not do as much good as one concrete suggestion about what to do when their child wets his pants or won't eat anything but peanut butter or smears feces on the wall.

At last I saw some signs of change in Jimmy. Not a "breakthrough" as when Anne Bancroft first holds Patty Duke's hand beneath the water pump, and she knows "wa wa" stands for what she drinks. But rather like a baby who finds out gradually that his babbled "oo's" and "ah's" are sounds he makes at his own will, and that he is in control.

I taught Jimmy a long "a" and an "e" and flipped his lower lip until he gave me "b" whenever I demanded it. I wanted him to say "baby," but when he tried to put it all together, it came out "badee" every time.

"Say bay."
"Bay."
"Say bee."
"Bee."
"Say baybee."
"Bayde."

For weeks we practiced that until one day "baby" exploded from his lips.

We marched around the building and opened doors to offices and showed off "baby" to anyone who'd listen. Jimmy knew he'd climbed a mountain. But Mount Everest was still ahead.

I held a rubber doll, the kind that wets after water is given by a plastic bottle. Each time he asked for "baby," and soon he said it without prompting. He loved the candy I provided and the pretzels and the raisins. I might have had success without food, but I wasn't taking any chances.

If you press his lips together, and the child utters anything, it will likely sound like "m." We practiced "m's" for M&M's, and he learned to ask for his rewards. The vowels were not so hard to teach and Jimmy soon had a repertoire of "ma," "mu," "me," "mo," "ba," "bu," "be," "bo." Put two "ma's" together, and Jimmy could label his mother. Two "ba's" are what a sheep says. A cow says "moo." "Who's a big boy?" "Me."

His behavior hadn't improved much, but I was optimistic now. His father worked with him at home and sometimes told me some brand new word that Jimmy said, so we could practice it at school.

His repertoire increased to "pot" and "pan" and "big" and "boat" and "more" and "my" and "pretty." We worked together from a deck of cards with simple drawings of animals or objects that he could recognize. These were sold at Woolworth's for a dollar and twenty-nine cents.

Poker chips replaced the candy as he grew more competent. Each time he said a word correctly, a chip was placed upon a card. The card had neatly ruled boxes, and when the card was filled, he got his reward.

The first time Jimmy put two words together was a thrill. A one word label is O.K., but it really doesn't sound like much. But two words is almost a sentence, and once a child does that, you know he'll talk someday. It didn't happen accidentally or out of the blue, but only after a hundred tries and my patience was a thread about to snap. "My daddy!" Soon after that I got "No more" (the candy was all gone), and later "Pretty box." Not perfect but recognizable.

What greater achievement can there be in life than the acquisition of a spoken language? Take that away and we are isolated. Can we think except by words? How much then can a wordless child learn? Can he reason or solve problems? How can we teach a child who has no tools to understand? And how does he, in turn, express his needs or vent his feelings? A people bind themselves together by their common language.

And so it is with families. Words are not taught formally but develop as we grow up around people who are speaking. We really don't know how it happens.

Some say it happens by conditioning, associations between the object and the word. Words are combined and sequenced and retained because they work, and the word almost becomes the thing. A chimp does not have the vocal mechanism to speak one word, but if you find an alternate method for response—like poker chips on a magnetic board—that chimp can compose sentences and answer questions. He even asks a few, provided he's been taught.

But others speculate that there may be some innate capacity to search for rules. The child hears a thousand different sentences until he acquires the grammar to compose his own. Who knows? But what starts out as an undifferentiated cry of hunger or pain, gives way to babbling as vocal play, then echolalic imitation of a sound. At last the repetitions acquire meaning, and by the time a child is six, we can no longer count the words he knows.

Yes, language is a talisman that lets us know a child is developing all right. The child of four, or even three, who does not talk presents a danger sign. There may be problems. Find out. Provide some help.

Yet few communities had programs for the special child below the age of six. And, what do you tell the parents of a child who doesn't talk? No one likes to be the first to say that something is amiss. So, if there is uncertainty, they wait and hope. "The child will talk when he is ready. Give him more time. Let nature take its course. No need for alarm."

And while we tried to educate, telling the world that waiting was the worst thing that could be done, a learned doctor advised in his syndicated column to worried parents to "wait and see." We wrote to him suggesting he was wrong but got no reply.

When at last the child is sent to see a specialist, sophisticated tests of reflexes or coordination or arousal are used—wooden blocks to fit in wooden holes: padded earphones to hear pure tones: stainless steel hammers to tap tendons: flashlights aimed into the pupil to watch the pupil dilate. We have norms for thousands of other three-year olds, so comparisons are possible. With all the skills and tricks and experience and armamentarium for our use, we try to choose between emotional and organic deficits, between childhood schizophrenia and mental retardation, between deafness and central auditory imperception, between, between, between.

But, such elegant distinctions are in vain if no one tries to teach the child to say a word or tells the parents what to do when their child wants water and can only grunt "uh." And all the fancy labels aren't worth a damn if another year or two goes by, and the child still won't talk.

Linguists believe there is a time to learn to speak, and if that time goes by, then chances become very poor that a child will speak at all. We took that seriously and structured our priorities. "Whatever else you do, teach language," we told our teachers. "And if this child does not learn to talk, you've failed."

We wrote out a curriculum and bound it into manuals. Each teacher in our program was made to follow the outline and check off what the child did learn and what he didn't. And, only children without language were accepted; we sent the others elsewhere.

We corralled whoever was available, so that every

child was seen for individual help every day. Volunteers and secretaries, college student interns, even psychologists became the language trainers. Each day the children were escorted, one by one, into a private room. Each day they practiced sounds until we saw a change and the sounds became syllables and syllables became words. The rest of us watched through the one-way mirrors and made notes.

The children were inhibited at first, their tiny chins buried in tiny shoulders and eyes filled with tears. We did our best to make the language pleasant with M&M's and pretzel sticks. Then, gradually, the inhibitions faded and the children ventured sounds. Then drill and practice and endless repetition, tedious and monotonous.

The parents read our manuals too. They worked along with us at home, then came in once a week for counseling. They brought their charts to show the progress, and we told them how well they were doing. Some brought tape recordings. We listened and made suggestions for new words to imitate, new ways to motivate. We gave support where many had despaired of their child ever talking. For most, our magic was effective. The children learned to say the words and put them into sentences. The parents learned they had more power than they thought. They could help their child to talk.

We learned to respect the parents of the handicapped and never once regarded them as neurotic. And, if we found them feeling guilty over what their unions had produced, or angry at the quirk of fate that damaged cells or twisted genes, then we could understand that too. And we could tell them to give up obsessive questioning about the cause and what if things had turned out differently or what will he be when he is twenty-five. Instead, we focused upon today.

"Handle tomorrow when it comes. Just get him to say 'Ma Ma' first, and we'll decide together what comes next. And don't think that because there are no letters after your name that you can't do this work. Most of the language training in the world is done by parents, not psychologists."

Jimmy went on to another program today. He knows some letters now, and he'll be reading soon. His articulation stinks, and we can't always understand everything he says. Once in a while, he still pulls off a shoe and grins. But he has progressed beyond the other kids, and I'm afraid he might be bored with those who hardly talk at all. So we're sending him on. He'll take with him the bus song and a predilection for candy and some spoiling. A year from now he won't remember us too well. But he says what he wants to say now, and asks "Why?"

19

Press the Ball, Billy

Billy and I were no strangers to each other. For months we had worked together at a simple game. I placed five cards on the five panels of a large board mounted on some steel shelving. One panel was correct because I had designated it so. I threw a switch so that, when depressed, the panel lit a row of lights and rang a bell. A picture was on every card. Often four of the panels had the same picture. Only the correct panel differed. We called this an oddity problem, and it was made simple to maximize the chances of success. Once mastered, I could vary the complexity of the discrimination task by varying other pictures as well.

"Press the ball, Billy," I commanded.

The order had to be direct, without ambiguity. Billy unerringly oriented himself toward the ball, ignoring the four other pictures on the panels. Again and again he responded precisely, even though the ball appeared unpredictably in all of the five panel positions. Clearly he had learned the discrimination. I recorded each trial accurately on a data form.

Next I switched the rules. A tree was now correct; the ball was wrong. For the first few trials Billy missed. Methodically he pushed each panel until he found the

169

right one. By the fifth trial his performance reached perfection.

Now I was ready for the test. Removing all the pictures but tree and ball, I alternated the command.

"Find the tree, Billy. . . . Find the ball, Billy."

Billy gave me just one glance that I now recognized as confusion. Walking toward the board, he began his aimless twirling. He flipped one hand against the other. I knew it was useless to proceed that day.

Billy was five years old and was diagnosed as severely retarded. Born prematurely, he stopped breathing on his second day of life. Before they got him going again, several minutes had gone by—several precious minutes when brain cells got no oxygen. As an infant he did not sleep at night, and banged his head against the crib. He did not walk till almost four. He did not talk at all. Sometimes he made a babbling sound that gave us hope. We'd shape that "duga duga" gibberish to something meaningful, we thought. It didn't work that way. The methods that we touted, which worked with other kids, had no effect on Billy. Sometimes he would make a noise like "elephant," or "Mom," and then someone would get excited, and we all would come to hear. But Billy never did it twice, and we learned to distrust such wish-fulfilling optimism. At five years of age Billy had developed less than the average one year old. He did not toilet or feed himself. He could not chew his food at all; his mother fed him mushy food from little Gerber's jars. He flipped his hands and twirled around. He stumbled when he walked and seemed oblivious to those around him. His father seemed embarrassed when he came to the class; his mother loved him but had had a nervous breakdown.

Billy came to preschool every day. For one whole year we repeated words to him and rewarded him for any meager sound with sugar water through a straw, or melted ice cream on a spoon, or strokes upon his cheek. Although he never learned to speak, we saw a little change. He seemed to recognize the things around him in the school, to be a little less involved in his own fantasy. He stopped the flipping and the twirling and the other ways of self-stimulation. The holes inside his lip were gone since he stopped biting there. He learned "stand up," "sit down," and "turn around." Sometimes he would come when called. That took a year.

I knew that something more was needed to reach this little boy. I had to find a way in which to make demands on him, demands so clearly defined that even he could understand. I had to tell him when he acted right, immediately and without room for doubt. And if I found a way to do these things, I then had to find a task that he could learn and guide him along the way inch by inch.

At first, Billy pressed the panels randomly. He seemed aroused by lights and bells, but there was no order to his efforts, no guiding principle. I made no progress in teaching him to find a "house" or "ball" or "bear." How could I get him to attend?

We found a raucous buzzer that pierced the air with noxious sound. I turned it on and Billy winced; he did not like that noise. I took his hand within my own and pressed his finger to a button and the sound stopped. Again I turned the buzzer on and guided Billy's hand. The third time was a solo trial, and he knew what to do. Next I placed him far across the room and flicked my switch to "ON." Without hesitation, Billy ran straight to the button and hit it skillfully. Then it became a game. Whenever I was ready to begin our daily trials, I turned that buzzer on full blast. Far down the hall, Billy sat vacantly in class, while other children learned to talk. He picked himself up from a chair and left the classroom, unannounced, and opened doors to find the way to turn that buzzer off. This was the first consistent behavior we saw from Billy in all the time we'd had him.

A hundred and twenty-five years ago, a man named Richards started teaching children who were called defectives or imbeciles. He wrote of one who neither walked nor spoke but lay on the floor, oblivious to those around. Richards read to him each day. Then one day Richards saw a flicker of recognition, an interest in him, the man who read words that meant nothing to the boy. "At last," he wrote, in prose so elegant it caused a stir at influential meetings. "At last I've found a fulcrum on which to place my lever." I thought we'd found our fulcrum, too.

"If he can find one buzzer, why not two?" I reasoned.

I found another sound, this time a bell, and placed it far across the room. With Billy placed between the buzzer and the bell, I alternated back and forth until he learned to make a choice and shut off whichever sound was on. He never got it wrong. Both bell and buzzer were powerful in motivating Billy. There were no other stimuli in school or home that could control his comings and his goings as well.

To make Billy more attentive to visual stimuli, we turned a light on every time the buzzer sounded. Light, as well as sound, went off when Billy pressed the button. Gradually, the buzzer was withdrawn until the light alone elicited response. Next, light became a picture—a pretty lady from the rotogravure, and we called her "Mommy." Whenever "Mommy" was presented, Billy did his thing. Soon light could be withdrawn, and Billy learned to press the picture when we said, "Find the Mommy." It took a month before he did that well.

Back to the panel board we went. This time with success. He learned to press a "house," a "boy," a "tree," a "dog." We found he could learn almost any picture shown this way and could ignore the ones that were not right.

The Billy that performed for us was unlike the one we'd come to know. Behavior that was orderly and predictable replaced the dream-like withdrawal of the past. Yet this was only true when he was at the board. At all other times, he seemed the same. I found that he obeyed some rules. Although I could not always know his ways, I was certain of one thing. The weird or bizzarre things he did were not arbitrary. When things were made too hard for him, or the choices too ambiguous, we saw the same old patterns emerge which we, in our ignorance, had labeled meaningless, autistic. But what they really meant was plain—poor programming had built-in failure.

But mostly we were gratified. In hundreds of trials, Billy performed and seemed to make some gains. When things did not go well for him, we found that he could cry.

Then progress hit a snag. No matter how well Billy learned to see the differences in things, he never once was able to link pictures with their names. Psychologists had talked of problems such as this. In some retarded and brain-injured kids, a "dissociation" may exist between sensory modalities. A child may hear and also see but cannot learn to code from one sense to another. Whatever sounds he hears cannot be connected to what he sees.

Determined to find a way, I drew a bright red arrow upon a plastic overlay and used it as a marker to make sure Billy knew the picture that was accurate. He learned to spot the arrow. No matter what I said to press, he'd always get it right, provided I first moved the arrow to point out the way.

"Suppose I make the arrow smaller until it fades away. He'll have to hear me then to find out what I want. It's just a matter of conditioning him to listen as well as see," I thought.

The arrow was then made to shrink until it was a small red spot, a point of ink no bigger than a dot. Still, Billy pressed with accuracy.

I held my breath and wiped the dot away and used the empty overlay. All there was to guide him was my voice. Again he found the stimulus but not because he heard the name. A tiny sheen of light reflected from the wiped plastic caught his eye. Despite an intellect so small I could not measure it, Billy had found a way to foul my plan.

It's six years later now, and Billy is far away in some state institution where they don't use panel boards. An old hat of his still lies in a forgotten box of toys downstairs. I came upon a spiral book last week on which someone had scrawled "Billy's words." If someone would only find a way to solve that coding problem, they'd learn to help the Billys of our world.

And, as I write this now, I have to ask myself why I didn't try "such and such." It might have worked.

20
On Being a Flutterbudget

> "The village they now approached was not built in a valley, but on top of a hill, and the road they followed wound around like a corkscrew, ascending the hill easily until it came to the town.
>
> "'Look out!' screamed a voice. 'Look out, or you'll run over my child!'
>
> "They gazed around and saw a woman standing upon the sidewalk nervously wringing her hands as she gazed at them appealingly.
>
> "'Where is your child?' asked the Sawhorse.
>
> "'In the house,' said the woman, bursting into tears; 'but if it should happen to be in the road, and you ran over it, those great wheels would crush my darling to jelly. Oh, dear! Oh, dear! Think of my darling child crushed to jelly by those great wheels!'" (Baum, 1910)

She was twenty years old, tall, dark, fair of face. She handed me the scribbled note from her physician.

"Please treat Mary for depression and obsessive thoughts."

The most upsetting thoughts related to her future marriage.

"What if I have a child who's retarded?" repeated over and over in her mind like a haunting tune. She could not turn it off, and, as she brooded about the possibilities, her level of anxiety approached a panic state.

The thoughts started shortly after she discussed the subject of mental retardation with her fiance. She'd learned about genetic defects in Psychology 201 and had done some reading on her own. (You can learn a lot from *Woman's Day* and *Family Health*.) At first the thoughts came infrequently, but soon increased. Now they intruded all the time. She wasn't sleeping nights and couldn't concentrate. Almost anything could bring them on; references to pregnancy, raising children, or menstrual periods. Later, other thoughts would come as well. "What if I have syphilis? What if I die before the wedding?"

Freud stressed the defensive function of obsessive thoughts, controlling levels of anxiety or substituting for some deep, unconscious wish. It originates, he said, from cruel and hostile impulses which our upbringing has forced us to repress. He who has wished evil unto others or lusted after some forbidden fruit, expects punishment for such thoughts in the form of misfortune threatening from without. Compulsive rituals and obsessive thoughts become associated with the anxiety from such malevolence and somehow lessen it. Just as the child, sorely criticized for being dirty, learns to wash, so does the adult learn rituals to restore a balance to his guilt. Even rats can learn to turn a wheel compulsively, if that wheel once turned off a source of pain.

Mary came from a religious family, but she was liberated. She practiced birth control and felt abortion was O.K. But you can't rid yourself of a thousand years of Italian Catholic heritage that easily. The Old World superstition intertwined with current dogma, and no ecumenical Pope was going to change what her parents knew was true. No one believes in magic any more. But magical thinking is a common trait. The obstetrician had to use some special methods before her mother became pregnant. The old fox told them she was a "miracle baby." Mary believed all this. Her grand-mother was a mystic. She took Mary to a tea leaf reader who diagnosed her problem. It seems she'd been bewitched. It was as good an explanation as any.

Mary's father had a terrible temper, and his wife and children learned to tread around him softly. He was a massive man and could easily frighten a little girl or even a grown woman. He didn't simply yell when he was angry; he had "fits." Mary's mother was a buffer between her and the old man. A family conspiracy kept secret anything that would displease him.

I pointed out the similarities between the way she acted toward the world and how she acted toward her dad. She seemed intent upon not doing anything that might hurt other people's feelings. She thought she had to be a saint to be well liked. But deep down there was always that nagging resentment that people took advantage of her. She couldn't ever stand up to her parents because they were so good to her. They gave her everything. She didn't like to be dependent, but how could she refuse such generosity. She was their only daughter, and they were well-to-do. But she became depressed about her worthlessness.

Certain family conditions establish climates which achieve control by arousing guilt. Persons raised in such a way may be more prone to "what if" thoughts. The confessional is a safety valve. It works, of course, or why would it have lasted?

A psychologist from Illinois says sin is more relevant than illness. A person who is guilty cannot be reassured. If his self-hate is justified, then he must

change his attitude—acting honestly until he really
feels he merits something better. The obsessive must
accept his impulses and learn to say, "It's O.K. to be
angry, and my sexy thoughts are normal." Then Super-
ego may relax its hold and leave him free once more.

I asked Mary to discuss her "secret" with her
boyfriend. She mustered up the nerve, and when " the
wash was all hung out," he didn't take it badly. It seems
he wasn't so lily pure himself. She felt a lot better about
things after that.

We then spent a lot of time discussing self-
assertion. She learned to recognize her martyr-like
denial of self-interest. When friends would make
unreasonable demands, she found she could say no, and
lightning didn't strike. She could talk back to her
boyfriend, too. They had some colossal rows, but she
felt better about herself.

Her obsessive thoughts came less often now, and
somehow she wasn't so upset by them. We agreed to
stop the therapy soon after that.

A year went by before I heard from her again. She
had married and things had gone well for a while. But
again the thoughts had started. "What if I am a homosexual? What if I am a schizophrenic? What if I cheat on
my husband?"

It didn't take much insight to see what had gone
wrong. Her husband had been drafted. Mary had
moved into an apartment that her parents owned. They
wouldn't accept rent from her. To top things off, that
mystic, superstitious grandmother had moved in to
keep her company.

This time we practiced saying "no" to requests that
were unreasonable and to disagree when she felt it
necessary. Grandmom moved out, and Mary got a job
and paid the rent. She blurted out the anger she felt to

her husband. He came home on leave more often after that. She learned that she was over-altruistic, and that people wouldn't reject her for doing what was right for her. She found she didn't have to be so "nice."

The thoughts stopped coming after a while. For, when she learned that she was competent and had worth, there was no longer any guilt to be absolved.

Not all flutterbudgets are guilty. Some are merely anxious. Seymour became one when he was only twelve. It wasn't thoughts that worried him but socks and shoelaces. Most kids have compulsive rituals some time or other in growing up, like touching every fencepost or wearing a lucky shirt to take exams, or "step on a crack and break your mother's back." Seymour had to tie his shoes whenever they felt even slightly loose and then hitch up his socks. He wore the ones with tight elastic bands that cut red marks on his legs, but still he had to hitch them up. He also had a need to repeat what he'd said when it came out imperfect by his unreasonable criteria. Before each repetition, he had to touch both knees.

Behaviorist or Freudian, it doesn't take a lot of smarts to guess that there was something about his legs which made Seymour worry.

The symptoms began some weeks before when an orthopedist poked and prodded his aching knee and talked about some surgery Seymour might need. But surgery might not be needed if he didn't exercise and allowed the knee to heal. Seymour was twelve, and doc assumed he'd have the self-control.

Well, Seymour had a pair of track shoes, and he knew that he was fast. He'd watched the Olympics on TV, and that was what he wanted. He also had a bicycle with ten speeds and a long banana seat. The other twelve year olds from up the street didn't care much about a bum knee and surgery. Seymour was the kid to beat at racing, and when he wouldn't run, they goaded him and called him names that questioned his masculinity. So, Seymour ran, and rode his bike as well. As if that wasn't enough to worry about, a teacher humiliated him at school.

Seymour had had a twin who died at birth. His parents were careful to explain they'd really only wanted one, so God had taken the other. They visited the grave site twice each year. Seymour wanted it kept immaculate; he brushed the dirt away with his hands.

I taught him ways he could reduce anxiety by breathing deeply and relaxing muscles. It helped a little but not enough. I asked the orthopedist to remove the conflict about running and riding bikes, which Seymour knew were dangerous. A plaster cast immobilized the knee. The kids could write their names on it. It didn't bend enough to ride a bike or run, and anyone could see that a kid wearing a cast can't race. We got Seymour a ping pong table, and he could beat his friends without jeopardizing his knee.

The hitching, tying, and the repeating stopped dramatically. Eventually the cast came off and he could run again.

> "'All of your troubles are due to 'ifs',' declared the Wizard. 'If you were not a Flutterbudget, you wouldn't worry . . .'
>
> "After they had ridden in silence for a while, Dorothy turned to the little man and asked:
>
> "'Do ifs really make Flutterbudgets?'
>
> "'I think the ifs help,' he answered seriously. 'Foolish fears and worries over nothing, with a mixture of nerves and ifs, will soon make a Flutterbudget of any one.'"
> (Baum, 1910)

21
The Seat of Learning

Joey's doing better now. He's in a special school for kids with learning problems. Not a school for retarded kids, but one for those who've had some difficulty in learning how to read or spell or can't seem to fathom decimals or find the least common denominator. Their IQ's are high enough, and they have plenty of smarts, but some may have a perceptual problem that makes the letters seem reversed. Or others, even though they hear OK, just cannot seem to process sounds. For some it is an emotional problem, and things become so tense at school they just stop trying. Their parents' yelling doesn't help, and punishment for poor reports, such as forbidding TV, just complicates matters and generates resentments that are not easy to undo. That's the way it was with Joey.

He started out in parochial school, the kind with fifty kids in a classroom and a teacher who's harrassed and has no time to deal with abnormality. And Joey was hyperactive. He couldn't sit in that small seat without fidgeting. Even fidgets weren't enough; he had to get up and walk around. You just don't do that in some classrooms.

The Sister believed him to be "bad." She gave him a special seat in front of the entire class. The kids all faced the blackboard. He faced them. She chose a monitor to watch Joey. Whenever he made a move that wasn't allowed, she ratted to the teacher. It kept him in line. But, by the time he reached first grade, the patterns were well learned. He hated school. He couldn't learn.

By third grade, things had gotten so bad he transferred to a public school. But he took his problems with him. He was two years behind in reading and arithmetic. He had a tutor every night and took medication for hyperactivity. Homework caused such bitter scenes of confrontation that his mother gave up in despair. His teacher seemed disinterested. He needed a special class, she said. She had no time to deal with him.

The family had their share of problems, too. Two older sisters had been in and out of hospitals. A younger brother seemed to be repeating Joey's problems in kindergarten. The parents were hardworking folk; they went to church on Sunday and were strict at home. Joey's mother yelled a lot. His father was a powerful man and didn't hesitate to use his hands across the backside of a child who had too fresh a mouth. But they were good people and wanted Joey to go to college someday. The sisters rebelled one by one, but they made out OK. The house was often noisy with arguments about the girls coming home late or making out in the living room. But basically the girls were not so different from their parents and so maintained their balance.

Joey seemed an ordinary kid except he said the others called him "mouse" at school because he was so quiet. He had nightmares, and many things were frightening. He didn't like the dark and always felt like he was being watched. He got sick quite frequently and needed to stay home from school. He wasn't making up lost ground that way. He was frightened when his father yelled and he hid in the closet to escape. "My father's a big gorilla," he said, "just like King Kong." He went to catechism class. They talked about death and hell and retribution. He loved to watch the horror movies on late night television.

His illnesses were mostly gastro-intestinal upsets. He was prone to constipation. I had my own ideas about the problems with his bowel. He told me that the seats in school were so hard his backside hurt so that he couldn't move his bowels. What better way to relate a somatic problem to anxiety over school? Sometimes he got so frustrated over his homework he pounded his fist against the wall.

Joey attended an "open classroom." It wasn't like the classrooms we had in P.S. 80 in the Bronx where teacher stands up in front of a blackboard reaching from wall to wall with beautifully stylized cursive letters on top. No one could ever imitate those letters, which made thousands of kids feel guilty. "Why can't mine look like that?" P.S. 80 wasn't run the same way either. Every kid in P.S. 80 was doing the same thing at the same time. Our teacher pitched her lessons to the average child. That's why it seemed advisable to change, so that each child could go at his own pace and learning could be individualized.

Such schools are using open classrooms now. The teacher hands out worksheets, and each child knows he's got to finish by a certain date. But then he's on his own to get things done. Sometimes he makes a contract with the teacher committing himself to certain goals. Sometimes he tells the teacher when he's ready to take the test. The teacher marks his progress on big charts with silver and gold stars.

The system worked well with most of Joey's class-mates, especially the clean-scrubbed, pigtailed girls who always understood about the fractions and decimal points and volunteered to clean the blackboard and raised their hands to answer questions. It didn't work so well for Joey who spent his time drawing airplanes and didn't do his SRA's and didn't worry much until the day before they all were due. Then he'd get sick. To make things worse he had no friends, and he was the one who got the teasing. He ate alone in the cafeteria, and once his lunch was thrown out the window. He was the only Italian kid in the class and was kind of scrawny. The kids knew a good name for Italians.

He told me once that he'd seen men from outer space. They'd landed in a rocket ship. Joey ran the other way. He wasn't crazy. He needed something going for him to build his ego. Something to tell the other kids and lord it over them for a change. Of course, no one believed him. I listened with interest to his tale and didn't challenge what he said. "Quite an adventure," I remarked.

I met a few times with Joey's father, King Kong, and told him what I thought was going wrong. He wasn't such a bad guy, after all, and he took the pressure off. We stopped the catechism lessons. That alone let me be Joey's friend. I asked his mother to be sure he went to school unless his fever was 100 degrees or more, and "enough already" with the late night monster show.

His teacher, who was critical, but never gave Joey special help or sent work home, was a more difficult nut to crack. The school psychologist lent a hand. He set up a daily report about behavior and attention and industry in school. The teacher filled it out, and Joey carried it home in his back pocket. There were rewards at home for minor accomplishments. The teacher made sure his assignment pad was in his knapsack every day at three. He had no more excuses about forgetting things.

We role played how to deal with the aggressive kids, and he actually had a fight or two and made some friends. The kids left his lunch alone after that. He joined the football squad. His mother sewed his numerals on and made him an equipment bag. His father came to watch the games.

Sometimes we had a family session. The older sisters came, and the younger brother made a pest of himself. But we weren't talking about Joey's behavior for a change. The teenage sisters were complaining about how unfair things were. Joey encouraged them to talk freely.

The stomach problems disappeared, and he went to school each day without a fuss. His work improved a little too, but not enough to bring him up to where he ought to have been.

A year went by, and he had another teacher. Things were rotten academically. We finally decided it was not working and got the necessary papers signed and sent away so he could be enrolled in a class where he would fit.

It used to be in P.S. 80 that children who were slow to learn were placed in the "Ungraded" class. That's what they called special education in the 1940's. That's where they placed the "dummies." They weren't all retarded, either. The public schools didn't have to take retarded kids. These were the kids who learned too slowly, and the class remained the same year after year. All ages were lumped together. Why hire more than one teacher? The kids wouldn't learn much anyway.

In the Junior High, classes were numbered by ability. The No. 1 class was the best, then No. 3 and No. 4 and so on down the line. You took a test to see which class you would be put into. The No. 2 class was the worst. It was numbered out of sequence so no one would suspect. Of course, it was no secret. The kids knew who was dumb.

Today, learning disability has become a fad. You

even see ads on TV, showing teachers with enough savvy to know that just because a kid has trouble doesn't mean that he is dumb. Trouble may result from some specific lesion in the brain that interferes with ways we process what we see or hear. Some call it minimal brain damage or MBD for short. The neurologists all know about it, and some educators have made a name by being expert in learning disability. Some have constructed tests that measure language or perception. The tests have special names like "auditory encoding" or "figure-ground perception," and when a child who can't read or write does poorly on these tests, they make a diagnosis. The special classes try to remediate the perceptual problem or bypass it. They haven't figured out which way is most appropriate. But there are motoric and visual and linguistic approaches to teaching. So now we have the learning specialists and self-styled experts and a hundred tests of minute processes and God knows where it all will end.

A psychologist in Montgomery County, Pennsylvania, whose head is screwed on right, has pointed out that the whole thing's circular, and it's a specious argument that intellect can be chopped up into such parts and reified as if there really was something concrete in the brain called "constancy of shape" or "auditory-vocal association." And I would like to know about the kids who learn to read and understand about partitioning of sets and adding exponents. How many of those really bright, well motivated, high achieving kids will also show some poor responses to the tests of learning disability? No one has ever really checked.

Despite all this, special education classes often seem to work. Not because of all the testing or the pseudoscientific theory or the self-styled experts, but because the classes are smaller and the teachers are better and the pressure is off. By identifying a problem and giving it a label, it helps the educators to understand and tolerate and do a little more for the Joeys of the world. Time will take its course, and he will learn. But not because of any special methods or techniques of so-called prescriptive teaching. The educational hocus pocus doesn't really exist.

Sometimes things don't turn out well, and kids get isolated from the normal school and locked into a system of nonachievement, and what was a minor adjustment problem then becomes a self-fulfilling prophecy. With Joey, it didn't seem to work that way. He liked his new school. He found some other kids who'd had a bad time in the regular classes. His reading level is still below average, but he's making steady progress now, and learning is no longer a pain in the behind.

22
Fancy That

We sat across the table from each other for the first time. I tried to structure my impressions of John so as to formulate a strategy for therapy. "He is fearful and insecure," his father had complained. "He can't compete with other kids and has no friends."

It took no more than a few minutes to confirm the father's description. Shy, inhibited, and timid, John had been over-protected by an anxious mother and over-controlled by a domineering father. Flabby and over-weight, it was clear John would be no physical match for the other twelve-year olds in his class.

"Let's play an imagination game," I suggested. "Your job is just to listen. Try to imagine what you hear as clearly as possible, as though it were really happening. Later I will ask you to make up stories too.

"Let's make believe that you are captain of the football team and the most popular boy in your class. During your last game you ran sixty yards to make the winning touchdown that clinched the league championship. After the game you had a date with the prettiest girl in the class. Right now you are walking home from school, and you happen to pass some tough kids picking on a younger student. They are taking his hat and rubbing it in the mud.

"'Give it back to him,' you command, 'or you'll be picking your teeth up from the ground!' 'Who's going to

make us?' the largest bully asks belligerently. 'I will!'
you answer, grabbing him by the collar."

The use of structured fantasy in psychotherapy is
based on the assumption that there is a relationship
between such fantasy and behavior. Freud said that
fantasy, like dreams, is wish-fulfilling and provides
access to the unconscious. So therapists use play techniques to encourage children to express their needs
freely and without fear. For instance, a well-known
child analyst worked with a child who'd had an extra
finger removed and who was also worried about a
tonsillectomy. The child built a cow stall with play
blocks and it was shaped like six appendages.

Fantasizing what we fear until no tension is
aroused makes it much easier to deal with frightening
situations. "Emotive imagery" is what one therapist
calls it. He asks the fearful and inhibited child to have a
fantasy imagining that he is Captain Midnight or
Superman and does brave deeds. The children learn to
be assertive in this way, he says. A not-too-orthodox
behaviorist in Boston makes alcoholics think of noxious
and nauseating images whenever they encounter alco-
hol or its accouterments.

I wrote a paper once about the role of fantasy. It
was a scholarly review of all the relevant research tries.
It showed that there was continuity between our
motives and our thoughts. A hungry person thinks of
food, and sexual arousal causes dreams so vivid their
imprint is left on sheets. The Harvard people knew all
that and made further tests to show that fantasy could
be a measure of such needs as power and achievement
and affiliation with our fellow man. TV arouses fantasy, and most agree that The Untouchables is more
potent fare than Mr. Rogers' Neighborhood. It's true

there is some controversy about whether TV stimulates the child toward aggressive roles or whether, by catharsis, it lessens such aggressive impulses. (My old psychology prof started that rhubarb, and it's not resolved yet.) If kids watch someone else being punished for what they might also do, they learn controls, even though they were never punished. So fantasy must play some role in learning inhibition.

I pointed out that affect is also fantasy-related. The way we interpret our physiological state may well depend on what we tell ourselves is going on. Subjects aroused internally by injections of adrenalin said they were angry or euphoric or afraid, depending upon what environmental cues were given them. A fantasy about a fearful stimulus, let's say a slimy snake, may make our insides behave almost exactly as they would if that serpent were wrapped around our neck.

A psychologist once defined a motive as anticipation of how we feel about a change. Our history conditions us to expect positive or negative effects with certain stimuli. We learn to approach situations which we expect to give us pleasure. We avoid what we expect to provide pain.

I postulated in my paper how fantasy arouses motives by changing expectations. John fears punishment for talking too loud or telling others what he thinks because he's never had the chance before. So, when I make him think about himself as strong or brave or arrogant, it might just have a chance of making him behave that way. The fantasy must be sufficiently intense to make him think of all the favorable consequences of doing what he previously feared. But, of course, if it's some behavior which is better off inhibited, the fantasy must make him think of what is negative, and in no uncertain terms.

I showed how fantasy invoked by therapists was an essential part of psychotherapy. Fantasy may be a powerful persuasive influence, I argued.

I wrote out all the arguments and carefully listed references, each in its proper form. But no one ever published it.

23

Peace at Any Price

Lester never smiled. Nine years old and already he had the world on his shoulders. His parents described his "mad" personality, his overly perfectionistic and serious temperament, and his chronic complaints. He didn't like the clothes he had to wear. He hated the school lunch no matter what it was. The weather never suited him; the work at school was rotten. The worst times were when he was asked to do something, like taking out the trash or cleaning up his room, or getting up for school on time. Lester didn't like to *have* to do anything. The most meager demands brought forth belligerence or tears. He was a mediocre student. He had almost no friends. Even kids could not stand him.

Lester's mother was a teacher. She dealt with children every day and should have known better. But somehow she never could forget the severe allergic problems Lester had had as an infant. The doctor didn't think he'd make it. He was strong as a gorilla now, but momma saw him as a fragile child. Father didn't know just what to do. A passive, mild man, he left decisions to his wife.

His parents were just never able to bring themselves to punish Lester. Their guilt was too intense.

Instead, they argued and cajoled and rationalized away
his rotten disposition. Their other child was well
adjusted, and they could punish *him*. But, then, he had
never been allergic, like Lester.

When Les was six, a child lived on their block who
went to a special school. People said that the child was
emotionally disturbed. Lester used to play with him,
and ever since that time, Lester's mother "knew" the
reason for Lester's temper tantrums—as if they could
be caught like chicken pox.

The family sat out in the waiting room. Lester sat
close to Mom for protection. I could sense her anxiety
and so could Lester. He began to cry when I asked him
to come in with me. Then he became angry when I
insisted.

I showed him some football cards, the kind that
come with bubble gum. I asked if he would help me to
complete a football pool. He forgot about his mother
for a moment and came in willingly. I got to know him
pretty well, and the next time he didn't resist.

I had some sessions with his parents, too.

"Let's not go pointing fingers," I advised. "We'll
concentrate on what's wrong now and see if we can
find a better way of dealing with things. What causes
you the most concern?"

"From the moment he awakens, he's cross and
irritable." Lester's father came alive with that statement.

"He won't get up when the alarm goes off, and he'd
be late for school if I didn't get him out of bed and dress
him every morning." That statement from his mother.
"I've got to help him with his homework, help him take
a bath and brush his teeth, help him practice clarinet
each day, and clean out the cage of his guinea pig. He
teases his brother constantly," she continued.

"But why must *you* do all these things?"

"I can't let him be late for school, or be held back, or go around like some disheveled cast-off, orphan child."

"Why not?"

I outlined for them a rule or two about how kids always find a way to gain attention.

"Lester provokes because it works," I said. "And he'll not stop as long as you persist in reasoning and arguing back and doing all the silly things you do to reward what is inappropriate and immature. You love your son, but you are really hurting him by not being strong enough to draw the line."

"It's true," the father said accusingly to the mother. "You never let me punish him the way I knew he needed to be punished. You wanted peace at any price, and you gave in and every year he got a little worse."

"What's done is done," I said. "You can't go back, but it's not irreversible. If you are willing to work with me and change how you behave, I think that things may soon improve."

When Lester was being pleasant, his parents were to talk with him with praise and recognition. But when he complained or whined, they were to turn their backs and walk away. If he overslept or pulled the sheets around his head, then they were to let him sleep even though he would be late. If he should miss the school bus, they were to let him walk rather than to frantically drive him to make the final bell. No more notes for the teacher to make everything all right.

We worked out an elaborate system of points with fines and bonuses. Good behavior was rewarded with a bonus and a record was kept by Lester in a balance book. His parents also signed the book. Whatever Lester did that Lester shouldn't do resulted in a fine. Credits and debits in separate columns were tallied up each night and brought forward on to the following page, as next day's starting balance. Points could be

spent each day for privileges like playing outside or
extra TV. But other points were "saved" toward purchasing a model plane or for a fishing trip. Tantrums
and destructive acts were "timed out" within a penalty
box where no one talked to him for ten minutes at a
time. This was repeated as needed. A negative balance
was not allowed. If he went in the red, he had to work
off what he owed by washing the car or mowing the
lawn. An "A" on a math test brought extra points. No
nagging or reminding were allowed. The parents were
to keep accounts but not to be emotional. Yelling and
cajoling never helped kids learn.

A family court was held each week, and Lester
could negotiate. His brother was included in the
scheme. They both had signed a contract with their
parents that I carefully prepared and duly witnessed. I
was designated as final arbitrator and appeal board for
the Family Court.

Why use a simple-minded system of points when
everybody knows that human interactions are complex? Because it teaches parents to do what works and
is a crutch that they can use until they see the results. It
takes away the choices and decisions they could not
make before. It gives them back responsibility for
dealing with their child, and when they see a change,
they learn that they still have the power to control. It
doesn't take long before they find they really don't need
points or stars or candy bars to keep an even keel.

Several months went by. Infrequent meetings and
a telephone call or two a month to make some minor
adjustments were all I had to do. Then Lester was
described by both his parents as "a new person." His
"moments" were now rare. He had grown up, they said.
He dressed himself each morning and arrived at school
on time. He stopped complaining. Once, when his

mother had a poison ivy rash, and the dishwasher wasn't working, Lester actually volunteered to do the dishes for the family. He mowed lawns to replace a storm window, accidentally broken. His grades in school improved. Four months later we agreed to drop the points.

"We've learned to make rules now and stick by them," his parents reported.

24

The Rabbi
and the
Psychologist

Religion was never a very important part of my childhood. Oh, I went to Hebrew School and learned to read well enough to follow the Saturday morning services. On Sunday morning we got Bible history and a smattering about holidays and festivals. When the time came I was bar mitzvah and made the usual speech thanking my parents. Instead of the traditional fountain pen, I received the latest writing sensation—a Reynolds twelve dollar ball point pen. It leaked all over my shirt pocket, and within a year you could buy it at Woolworth's for less than a dollar. My parents followed the dietary laws and lit the Sabbath Candles, but this was done without a great deal of understanding or feeling for the religion. So when the bar mitzvah was finished and the checks properly banked and thank you notes dutifully written, no one really expected me to continue Hebrew studies or attend Saturday services. For almost three decades Jewishness for me was little more than an occasional wedding, bar mitzvah, or funeral service, and a vague nostalgia on Rosh Hashannah and Yom Kippur.

It's likely that's as far as it would have gotten had I not had children of my own. In our not-too-Jewish neighborhood, Jackie was the only Jewish kid in her class. It became embarrassing when each year she was singled out to talk about whatever Jewish holiday was current. So we made the frantic phone calls to more religious friends and borrowed a *menorah* or a *dredel* and read up on the meaning of the day so Jackie could make her report.

When Bonnie and I finally decided the kids required a sense of identification that we could not provide, we took the easy way out. We affiliated with a reform synagogue led by a young, charismatic rabbi, well known for his ecumenical leanings, his outspoken convictions that religion should keep up with the times, and that people could "do their own thing" and still be good Jews. While he is not the rabbi in my story, his brand of Judaism influenced the generally lax religious climate in my family.

It was with no small degree of hesitation that I agreed to treat the eight-year old daughter of another rabbi, the orthodox Rabbi Myers. It wasn't that rabbis couldn't have problem children or harbor their own psychological problems. But I had doubts about being effective with a man whom I was certain would be strict in his religious observance, possibly rejecting of my religious persuasions, and accustomed to moralistic, philosophical and intellectual approaches to life.

Of course, these were only preconceptions on my part, but he more than lived up to them. Rabbi Myers believed in the letter of the law, even if the law dated back five thousand years. No matter if pigs were no longer fed garbage, Rabbi Myers found a reason not to eat *trayfe*. He saw himself as father to his congregation who, like children too young to make decisions for themselves, required his guidance and enlightenment concerning the teachings of the Talmud. Those who would change the religion of our forefathers were a danger to its very future. Those who denied their religion or were ashamed of it were worthy of his contempt. The males in his household wore *yarmulkes*, the traditional skullcap of the synagogue. His children were in a special religious school. Three hours every morning were devoted to the standard academic curriculum in English. Four hours each afternoon were devoted to the study of Hebrew. Saturdays were spent in reading and study, and Sunday morning was a schoolday. He wanted to maintain, he said, a culture within a culture—to protect his children as well as he could from outside influences. Perhaps someday they'd move to Israel. I wondered whether even there, where Yom Kippur, the holiest of days, yields the largest beach attendance of the year, the Myers might have difficulty maintaining their own culture.

Rebecca pulled against her father's arm as he tried to guide her into the office. Burying her face into his jacket, so as to avoid my glance, her tears were the Niagara Falls—no, the Red Sea. "I don't want to, *Abba*," she implored her father, the rabbi. Soothingly, the father, as with his congregation, comforted and cajoled. Gently, he urged her to cooperate, and hinted at wondrous delights at the Dairy Queen when we were done.

Rebecca was doing badly at the religious school. She was a year or two behind in reading and arithmetic. She hardly spoke at all and had made no friends. The teacher felt Rebecca needed a special school, and made it clear she knew something of family counseling. I wished she knew a little more of teaching.

The psychologist who'd seen Rebecca at the clinic

found a borderline intelligence. The parents knew that wasn't true, but they were worried. Rebecca hadn't cooperated at all.

The rabbi's efforts notwithstanding, Rebecca wasn't going to capitulate on that first visit. She stood against the door of the office, her face turned to the wall. Occasionally, she sneaked a bitter glance in my direction. Not a word would she utter.

"Wait, Rabbi," I counseled benignly. "Rebecca doesn't have to talk to me if she doesn't want to. I understand how angry and upset she is. You and I and *Ema* will talk. Next week perhaps she'll feel like talking, too."

Next week it was the same. The following week I took them all to the Dairy Queen. She accepted the chocolate frosty I offered conciliatorily but never once looked in my direction.

"Perhaps I might come visit you at home," I suggested. "Then we would become friends."

For the first time she looked me squarely in the eye. At last a breakthrough, I reasoned, and waited for her first words to me.

"If you come to my house, I will run up to my room and lock the door. I'll turn on the TV and the air conditioner so that I cannot hear you and I'll stay there till you leave."

And that's the way it went.

If you can't raise the bridge, lower the river.

I was able to discuss Rebecca with her parents as a negative, rebellious girl. They recognized their role in supporting Rebecca's opposition. They saw how their concern about her rebellion had led them to indulge her moodiness, and they were able to get a little tougher in setting limits and saying, "No!"

We came to the time when the rabbi could admit

what he had known all along—that the ultra-religious school with all the values and traditions that were so vital to his family just wouldn't work for Rebecca. And once he reached a decision that only a secular school could provide the help for learning disability, things began to happen quickly.

The boys in her new class didn't wear *yarmulkes*, and no one said the *borucha* before meals in that school cafeteria. And she wasn't the only one who had trouble with phonetics, so the teacher didn't look at her like teaching her was beneath her dignity. Rebecca was the only Jewish child, and she liked to tell the story of Chanukah. The little capsule so carefully built around her had finally been punctured. Even the rabbi became enthusiastic about the teacher who reached out to Rebecca and he looked the other way when she taught Rebecca "Silent Night." Hadn't the teacher also taught *Adon Olom?*

I tended to enjoy my sessions with the family. Sometimes the rabbi talked about religion. That was not the primary reason for our meeting, of course, but religion was his life, and he needed to maintain his role, just as I did mine. I saw no need for undermining that.

"Rabbi," I once teased, "on Yom Kippur our Reform Rabbi brought a rubber chicken into the synagogue and swung it around his head. It was his way of illustrating an old Jewish New Year's custom of killing a chicken to symbolically cast away one's own sins."

"He shouldn't make fun," he responded angrily. "I do something similar. It's symbolic. There's nothing old fashioned about it."

I wasn't going to reform the rabbi, and he wasn't going to get me to wear a skullcap and stop working on *Shabbos*. But Rebecca was coming out of her shell and doing better in reading.

"You know," the rabbi told me one day, "psychologists do God's work. Not all religion is in the synagogue."

Somehow that meant a lot to me.

References

Chapter 1

Doll, E.E. (Ed.), Historical review of mental retardation, 1800-1965. A symposium. *American Journal of Mental Deficiency*, 1967, 72, 165-189.

Doll, E.E. Historical survey of research and management of mental retardation in the U.S. In E.E. Trapp & P. Himelstein (Eds.), *Readings on the exceptional child: Research and theory*. New York: Appleton-Century-Crofts, 1962.

Fernald, W.E. Thirty years progress in the care of the feeble-minded. *Journal of Psycho-Asthenics*, 1924, 29, 206-219.

Haskall, R.H. Mental deficiency over a hundred years. *American Journal of Psychiatry*, 1944, 100, 107-118.

Itard, J. M. G. *De l'education d'un homme sauvage*. Paris: Goujon, 1801.

Kanner, L. *A history of the care of the mentally retarded*. Springfield, Ill.: Thomas, 1967.

Rosen, M., Clark, G.R., & Kivitz, M.S. *The history of mental retardation: Collected papers*. Baltimore: University Park Press, 1975.

Sequin, E. *Idiocy: And its treatment by the physiological method*. New York: Columbia University Press, 1907.

Skeels, H.M. & Dye, H.B. A study of the effects of differential stimulation on mentally retarded children. *Proceedings and addresses of the American Association on Mental Deficiency*, 1939, 44, 114-136.

Tyor, P.L. *Segregation or surgery: The mentally retarded in America, 1850-1920*. Doctoral Dissertation, Northwestern University, 1972, University Microfilms, Ann Arbor, Michigan.

Chapter 2

Rosen, M. *Valence, expectancy and dissonance reduction in the prediction of achievement striving*. Doctoral Dissertation, University of Pennsylvania, 1961.

Wishner, J. The concept of efficiency in psychological health and in psychopathology. *Psychological Review*, 1955, 62, 69-80.

Wishner, J. Efficiency in schizophrenia. *Bulletin de l'Association Internationale de Psychologie Appliquie*, 1965, 14, 30-47.

Chapter 3

Beck, S.J. *Rorschach's test. Basic processes.* Volume 1. New York: Grune & Stratton, 1944.

Klopfer, B., Ainsworth, M.D., Klopfer, W.C., & Holt, R.R. *Developments in the Rorschach technique.* Volume 1. New York: Harcourt, Brace & World, 1954.

Piotrowski, Z.A. *Perceptanalysis: A fundamental reworked, expanded and systematic Rorschach method.* New York: Macmillan, 1957.

Chapter 4

Bibring, E. The mechanism of depression. In P. Greenacre (Ed.), *Affective disorders: Psychoanalytic contributions to their study.* New York: International University Press, 1953, pp. 13-48.

Ferster, C.B. A functional analysis of depression. *American Psychologist,* 1973, 28, 857-870.

Gantt, W.H. *Experimental basis for neurotic behavior.* New York: Hoeber, 1944.

Laing, R.D. *The politics of experience.* New York: Ballantine, 1967.

Chapter 5

Boring, E.G. *A history of experimental psychology.* New York: Appleton-Century, 1929.

Ehrenwald, J. *From medicine man to Freud.* New York: Dell, 1956, p. 119.

Jourard, S.M. *Personal adjustment: An approach through the study of healthy personality.* Second Edition. New York: Macmillan, 1963.

Maslow, A.H. *Motivation and personality.* New York: Harper, 1954, p. 115.

Shaffer, L.F. & Shoben, E.J. *The psychology of adjustment: A dynamic and experimental approach to personality and mental hygiene.* Boston: Houghton Mifflin, 1956.

Szasz, T.S. The myth of mental illness. *American Psychologist,* 1960, 15, 113-118.

Torrey, E.F. What western psychotherapists can learn from witch-doctors. *American Journal of Orthopsychiatry,* 1972, 42, 69-76.

Zilboorg, G. & Henry, G.W. *A history of medical psychology.* New York: Norton, 1941.

Chapter 6

Rosen, M. Alice in Rorschachland. *Journal of Personality Assessment,* 1973, 37 (2), 115-121.

Chapter 7

Murray, H.A. *Explorations in personality.* New York: Wiley, 1938.

Chapter 8

Ayllon, T. The application of reinforcement theory to ward problems. Unpublished doctoral dissertation, University of Houston, 1959.

Ayllon, T. & Michael, J. The psychiatric nurse as a behavioral engineer. *Journal of Experimental Analysis of Behavior,* 1959,2, 323-334.

Dollard, J. & Miller, N.E. *Personality and psychotherapy: An analysis in terms of learning, thinking and culture.* New York: McGraw-Hill, 1950.

Freud, S. *The problem of anxiety.* Trans, H.A. Bunker from *Hemmung Symptom und Angst,* 1926. New York: Norton, 1936.

Jones, M.C. The elimination of children's fear. *Journal of Experimental Psychology,* 1924, 7, 383-390.

Miller, N.E. & Dollard, J. *Social learning and imitation.* New Haven: Yale University Press, 1944.

Skinner, B.F. *The behavior of organisms.* New York: Appleton-Century-Crofts, 1938.

Skinner, B.F. *Science and human behavior.* New York: Macmillan, 1953.

Watson, J.B. *Psychology from the standpoint of a behaviorist.* Philadelphia: Lippincott, 1919.

Watson, J.B. & Raynor, R. Conditioned emotional reactions. *Journal of Experimental Psychology,* 1920, 3, 1-14.

Wolpe, J. *Psychotherapy by reciprocal inhibition.* Stanford: Stanford University Press, 1958.

Wolpe, J. & Lazarus, A.A. *Behavior therapy techniques.* New York: Pergamon, 1967.

Chapter 9

Azrin, N.H., Sneed, T.J., & Foxx, R.M. Dry-bed training: Rapid elimination of childhood enuresis. *Behaviour Research and Therapy,* 1974, 12, 147-156.

Foxx, R.M. & Azrin, N.H. Dry pants: A rapid method of toilet training children. *Behaviour Research and Therapy,* 1973, 11, 435-442.

Lovibund, S.H. *Conditioning and enuresis.* New York: Macmillan, 1964.

Morgan, J.J.B. Treatment of enuresis by the conditioned reaction technique. *Psychological Bulletin*, 1938, 35, 632-633.

Morgan, J.J.B. & Witmer, F.J. The treatment of enuresis by the conditioned reaction technique. *Journal of Genetic Psychology*, 1939, 55, 59-65.

Mowrer, O.H. & Mowrer, W.M. Enuresis—a method for its study and treatment. *American Journal of Orthopsychiatry*, 1938, 8, 436-459.

Chapter 10

Lovaas, O.I., Schaeffer, B., & Simmons, J.Q. Experimental studies in childhood schizophrenia: Building social behavior in autistic children by use of electric shock. *Journal of Experimental Research in Personality*, 1965, 1, 99-109.

Solomon, R.L. Punishment. *American Psychologist*, 1964, 19, 239-253.

Tate, B.G. & Baroff, G.S. Aversive control of self-injurious behavior in a psychotic boy. *Behaviour Research and Therapy*, 1966, 4, 281-287.

Chapter 11

Challas, G., Chapel, J.L., & Jenkins, R.L. Tourette's disease: Control of symptoms and its clinical course. *International Journal of Neuropsychiatry*, 1967, 3, Suppl. 1, 95-109.

Killman, D.H. Gilles de la Tourette's disease in children: A review of the literature. *Journal of Child Psychology and Psychiatry*, 1965, 6, 219-226.

Rosen, M. & Wesner, C. A behavioral approach to Tourette's syndrome. *Journal of Consulting and Clinical Psychology*, 1973, 41 (2), 308-312.

Shapiro, A.K., Shapiro, E., Wayne, H., & Clarkin, J. The psychopathology of Gilles de la Tourette's syndrome. *American Journal of Psychiatry*, 1972, 129, 427-434.

Chapter 12

Jacobsen, E. *Progressive relaxation.* Chicago: University of Chicago Press, 1938.

Lang, P.J. & Lazovik, A.D. Experimental desensitization of a phobia. *Journal of Abnormal and Social Psychology*, 1963, 66, 519-525.

Lang, P., Lazovik, A.D., & Reynolds, D.J. Desensitization, suggestibility and pseudotherapy. *Journal of Abnormal and Social Psychology*, 1965, 70, 395-402.

Leitenberg, H., Agras, W.S., Barlow, D.H., & Oliveau, D.C. Contribution of selective positive reinforcement and therapeutic instructions to systematic desensitization therapy. *Journal of Abnormal Psychology,* 1969, 74, 113-118.

Paul, G.L. *Insight versus desensitization in psychotherapy.* Stanford: Stanford University Press, 1966.

Paul, G.L. & Shannon, D.T. Treatment of anxiety through systematic desensitization in therapy groups. *Journal of Abnormal Psychology,* 1966, 71, 124-135.

Rachman, S. Studies in desensitization: The separate effects of relaxation and desensitization. *Behaviour Research and Therapy,* 1966, 4, 7-16.

Wolpe, J. *Psychotherapy by reciprocal inhibition.* Stanford: Stanford University Press, 1958.

Wolpe, J. & Lazarus, A.A. *Behavior therapy techniques: A guide to the treatment of the neuroses.* New York: Pergamon Press, 1966.

Chapter 13

Clark, G.R., Kivitz, M.S., & Rosen, M. *A transitional program for institutionalized adult retarded.* Project No. 1275-P, Vocational Rehabilitation Administration, Department of Health, Education and Welfare, 1968.

Rosen, M. & Floor, L. Investigating the phenomenon of helplessness in the mentally subnormal. *American Journal of Mental Deficiency,* 1975, 79 (5), 565-572.

Rosen, M., Floor, L., & Baxter, D. The institutional personality. *British Journal of Mental Subnormality,* 1971, 17, 2-8.

Rosen, M., Floor, L., & Baxter, D. Prediction of community adjustment: A failure of cross-validation. *American Journal of Mental Deficiency,* 1972, 77, 111-112.

Rosen, M., Floor, L., & Zisfein, L. Investigating the phenomenon of acquiescence in the mentally handicapped: I. Theoretical model, test development, and normative data. *British Journal of Mental Subnormality,* 1974, 20, Part 2 (39), 58-68.

Rosen, M., Floor, L., & Zisfein, L. Investigating the phenomenon of acquiescence in the mentally handicapped: II. Situational determinants. *British Journal of Mental Subnormality,* 1974, 21, Part 1 (40), 6-9.

Rosen, M., Kivitz, M.S., Clark, G.R., & Floor, L. Prediction of post-institutional adjustment of mentally retarded adults. *American Journal of Mental Deficiency,* 1970, 74, 726-734.

Wilkie, E.A., Kivitz, M.S., Clark, G.R., Byer, M. & Cohen, J.

Developing a comprehensive rehabilitation program within an institutional setting. *Mental Retardation*, 1968, 6, 35-39.

Chapter 14

Rosen, M. Independence for the mentally retarded. *Intellect*, 1975, 103 (2364), 371-375.

Chapter 15

Clark, G.R., Bussone, A., & Kivitz, M.S. Elwyn Institute's Community Living Program. *Challenge*, 1974, 17 (2), 14-15.

Clark, G.R., Kivitz, M.S., & Rosen, M. From custody to independence: Report of a rehabilitation program for retarded adults at Elwyn Institute. *Rehabilitation Record*, 1970, 11, 10-12.

Clark, G.R., Kivitz, M.S., & Rosen, M. From research to community living. *Human Needs*, 1972, 1 (1), 25-28.

Rosen, M., Zisfein, L., & Hardy, M. The clinical application of behavior modification technique: Three case studies. *British Journal of Mental Subnormality*, 1972, 18, Part 2 (35), 1-8.

Chapter 16

Bass, M.S. Marriage for the mentally deficient. *Mental Retardation*, 1964, 2 (2), 45-48.

Davison, G.C. Elimination of a sadistic fantasy for a client-controlled counterconditioning technique: A case study. *Journal of Abnormal Psychology*, 1968, 73, 84-89.

de la Cruz, F.F. & LaVeck, G.D. (Eds.), *Human sexuality and the mentally retarded*. New York: Brunner/Mazel, 1973.

Feldman, M.P. Aversion therapy for sexual deviations: A critical review. *Psychological Bulletin*, 1966, 65, 65-79.

Ferster, C.B. Reinforcement and punishment in the control of homosexual behavior by social agencies. In H.J. Eyesenck (Ed.), *Experiments in behaviour therapy*. London: Pergamon, 1965, pp. 189-207.

Floor, L., Baxter, D., Rosen, M., & Zisfein, L. A survey of marriages among previously institutionalized retardates. *Mental Retardation*, 1975, 13 (2), 33-37.

Floor, L., Rosen, M., Baxter, D., Horowitz, J., & Weber, C. Sociosexual problems in mentally handicapped females. *Training School Bulletin*, 1971, 68, 106-112.

Gordon, S. *Facts about sex for today's youth*. New York: John Day, 1973.

Kempton, W. *A teacher's guide to sex education for persons with learning disabilities*. North Scituate, Mass.: Duxbury Press, 1975.

Rosen, M. Conditioning appropriate heterosexual behavior in mentally and socially handicapped populations. *Training School Bulletin*, 1970, 66, 172-177.

Rosen, M. Psychosexual adjustment of the mentally handicapped. In M.S. Bass (Ed.), *Sexual rights and responsibilities of the mentally retarded.* Proceedings of the Conference of the American Association on Mental Deficiency, Region IX, University of Delaware, Newark, Del., October 12-14, 1972.

Chapter 17

Birnbrauer, J.S., Bijou, S.W., Wolf, M.M., & Kidder, J.D. Programmed instruction in the classroom. In L. Ullmann & L. Krasner (Eds.), *Case studies in behavior modification.* New York: Holt, Rinehart & Winston, 1965.

Rosen, M. Behavior modification. In R. Hyatt & N. Rolnick (Eds.), *Teaching the mentally handicapped child.* New York: Behavioral Publications, 1974.

Sidman, M. & Stoddard, L.T. Programming perception and learning for retarded children. In N.R. Ellis (Ed.), *International review of research in mental retardation.* Vol. I. New York: Academic Press, 1966, pp. 152-158.

Chapter 18

Bricker, W.A. & Bricker, D.D. A program of language training for the severely language handicapped child. *Exceptional Children,* 1970, 37, 101-111.

Brown, R. The acquisition of language. *Disorders of Communication,* 1964, 42.

Lovaas, O.I. A program for the establishment of speech in psychotic children. In J.K. Wing (Ed.), *Early Childhood Autism.* London: Pergamon, 1966, pp. 115-144.

McNeill, D. The capacity for language acquisition. *Volta Review,* 1966, 852, 5-21.

Rosen, M., Wesner, C., Richardson, P., & Clark, G.R. A pre-school program for promoting language acquisiton. *Hospital & Community Psychiatry,* 1971, 22, 280-282.

Skinner, B.F. *Verbal behavior.* New York: Appleton-Century-Crofts, 1957.

Chapter 19

Hermelin, B., & O'Connor, N. Like and cross modality responses in normal and subnormal children. *Quarterly Journal of Experimental*

Psychology, 1960, 12, 48-53.

Luria, A.R. *The role of speech in the regulation of normal and abnormal behavior.* London: Pergamon Press, 1961.

Rosen, M., Kivitz, M. & Rosen, B.S. Uni-modal and cross-modal "coding" in the mentally retarded. *American Journal of Mental Deficiency,* 1965, 69 (5), 716-722.

Rosen, M., Wesner, C., Richardson, P., & Clark, G.R. A pre-school program for promoting language acquisition. *Hospital and Community Psychiatry,* 1971, 22 (9), 280-282.

Rosen, M., Zisfein, L., & Hardy, M. The clinical application of behavior modification techniques: Three case studies. *British Journal of Mental Subnormality,* 18, Part 2 (35), 1-8.

Chapter 20

Baum, L.F. *The Emerald City of Oz.* New York: Random House, 1910, p. 242.

Freud, S. *Psychopathology of everyday life.* Sixth edition. New York: Mentor, 1958.

Hodgson, R., Rachman, S., & Marks, I. The treatment of chronic obsessive-compulsive neurosis: Followup and further findings. *Behaviour Research and Therapy,* 1972, 10, 181-189.

Marks, I.M. New approaches to the treatment of obsessive-compulsive disorders. *Journal of nervous and mental disease,* 1973, 156, 420-426.

Mowrer, O.H. Sin, the lesser of two evils. *American Psychologist,* 1960, 15, 302-304.

Rachman, S., Hodgson, R., & Marks, I.M. Treatment of chronic obsessive-compulsive neurosis. *Behaviour Research and Therapy,* 1971, 9, 237-247.

Rosen, M. A dual model of obsessional neurosis. *Journal of consulting and clinical psychology,* 1975, 43 (4), 453-459.

Chapter 21

Kirk, S.A. & Bateman, B. Diagnosis and remediation of learning disabilities. *Exceptional Children,* 1962, 29, 73-78.

Mann, L. & Phillips, W.A. Fractional practices in special education: A critique. *Exceptional Children,* 1967, 33, 311-319.

McCarthy, J.J. & McCarthy, J.F. *Learning disabilities.* Boston: Allyn & Bacon, 1969.

Chapter 22

Bandura, A., Grusec, J.E., & Menlove, F.L. Vicarious extinction of avoidance behavior. *Journal of Personality and Social Psychology*, 1967, 5, 16-23.

Erikson, E.H. *Childhood and society.* New York: Norton, 1963.

Feshbach, S. The drive-reducing function of fantasy behavior. *Journal of Abnormal and Social Psychology*, 1955, 50, 3-11.

Feshbach, S. The stimulating vs. cathartic effects of vicarious aggressive activity. *Journal of Abnormal and Social Psychology*, 1961, 63, 381-385.

Kelly, G.F. Guided fantasy as a counseling technique with youth. *Journal of Counseling Psychology*, 1972, 19, 355-361.

Lazarus, A.A. & Abramovitz, A. The use of "emotive imagery" in the treatment of children's phobias. In L.P. Ullmann & L. Krasner (Eds.), *Case Studies in Behavior Modification.* New York: Holt, Rinehart & Winston, 1966, pp. 300-304.

McClelland, D.C. Notes for a revised theory of motivation. In D.C. McClelland (Ed.), *Studies in Motivation.* New York: Appleton-Century-Crofts, 1955, pp. 226-234.

Schachter, S. The interaction of cognitive and physiological determinants of emotional state. In L. Berkowitz (Ed.), *Advances in Experimental Social Psychology*, Vol. I. New York: Academic Press, 1964, pp. 49-80.

Chapter 23

Patterson, G.R. & Gullion, M.E. *Living with children.* Champaign, Ill.: Research Press, 1968.

Rosen, M., Zisfein, L. & Hardy, M. The clinical application of behavior modification techniques: Three case studies. *British Journal of Mental Subnormality*, 1972, 18, Part 2 (35), 1-8.

Index